The Twelve Christ Chose

From Jerusalem, men, twelve in number, went out into the world; and although unlearned and without talent of speech, they have, through the power of God, made the whole race of men to understand that they have been sent out by Christ to teach the word of God to all.

JUSTIN MARTYR, *Apologia* 1:39; *ca.* 153 A.D.

In these days he went out into the hills to pray; and all night he continued in prayer to God. And when it was day, he called his disciples, and chose from them Twelve, whom he named apostles; Simon, whom he named Peter, and Andrew his brother, and James and John, and Philip, and Bartholomew, and Matthew, and Thomas, and James the son of Alphaeus, and Simon who was called the Zealot, and Judas the son of James, and Judas Iscariot, who became a traitor.

LUKE 6:12–16

The Twelve Christ Chose

by

ASBURY SMITH

HARPER & BROTHERS
NEW YORK

THE TWELVE CHRIST CHOSE

Printed in the United States of America

Library of Congress catalog card number: 58-7103

To Rachel
whose love is
a constant inspiration

Contents

The Twelve Christ Chose

The woodcuts of the Apostles which appear at the beginning of chapters were cut about 1583 by the Italian artist Agostino Carracci (1557–1602). He followed the custom of the period in omitting Judas. The illustrations are reproduced here with the permission of The Metropolitan Museum of Art, New York. The publishers are grateful to the staff of the Print Collection at the Museum for advice in the selection of these prints.

1
These Twelve

SO VAGUE IS OUR KNOWLEDGE OF THE APOSTLES THAT even competent Bible students sometimes find themselves pressed to name the Twelve our Lord chose to be with him. For most of us the Twelve are figures in a stained-glass window, and if the names on the windows were interchanged we would never know the difference. A representation of Andrew could serve quite as well for James, or, indeed, an aged man with a long beard and a kindly face could pass for any of the Twelve save Judas.

Added to this lack of individuality is the tendency to separate the Twelve from common humanity by making them saints. A saint, to most of us, is a person whose relations with God and man have been perfected. He is beyond our reach. But Paul had no such concept when he wrote of the members of the church in Corinth, "Those consecrated in Christ Jesus, called to be saints together with all those who in every place call on the name of our Lord Jesus Christ, both their Lord and ours."

When the citizens of Lystra, awed by the healing of a sick man, tried to worship Paul, he cried out in protest, "We also are men, of like nature with you." If the stained-glass figures of the apostles could be given voice, they would echo Paul's words, "We are men of like nature with you." However, this fact of their humanity should in no way lessen our admiration for these great men. The more we appreciate their humanity and their individual differences, the more we appreciate the qualities that made them grow in grace and in knowledge of our Lord Jesus Christ. Only as the Word becomes flesh, only as the Divine clothes itself in the human, can we understand God's will and way.

The Twelve whom Jesus chose were no doubt young men. Jesus died at the age of thirty-three, and it is doubtful if any of his disciples were much older than he was at the time of his death. John may have been no more than eighteen at the time he was called to discipleship. Greatness is frequently equated with age, but Albert Einstein published his theory of relativity at the age of twenty-six. At twenty, Alexander Hamilton was one of Washington's staff officers and at thirty he published his essays on government in the *Federalist*, essays that Guizot called the greatest work he knew "in its application of elementary principles of government to practical administration." When Francis Asbury was twenty-six, John Wesley sent him to America "to spread scriptural holiness over the land." The apostles, too, were probably young men, eager, alert, creative.

Another characteristic common to the apostles is that they came from the common walks of life. Four were fishermen; one was a tax collector. There was not a priest or a member of the clergy in their ranks. Not one of them had received professional ecclesiastical training. It is an open question whether all of the Twelve could read and write. Only three have left any written record behind them. Historically, some of the most vital religious awakenings have come through unordained, theologically untrained persons. From the prophets of Israel to the unordained local preachers of certain modern denominations, the Holy Spirit has often used unofficial channels through which to work. The new wine of God keeps breaking out of the old wineskins. "This was the Lord's doing and it is marvelous in our eyes."

Four of the twelve apostles came from two families. Peter and Andrew were brothers; James and John were sons of Zebedee. Five of the disciples, Peter, Andrew, James, John, and Philip, were followers of John the Baptist before they became followers of Jesus. James the son of Alphaeus and Simon Zealot are unknown except in name. All of the disciples except Judas Iscariot came from Galilee.

The apostles chosen differed temperamentally. Peter was an impulsive man ruled by his emotions; Thomas was a realist who faced every situation cautiously. Andrew was friendly, reaching out for fellowship; Judas went his way alone, a man of mystery. This difference in temperament has tended to make each apostle a symbol of his dominant characteristic. The method has advantages in presenting moral truth, but it is not the best way to understand fully a various group of many-sided men.

In the Scripture the material on the apostles has many apparent contradictions and omissions. In studying this record it should be remembered that well-known persons are at best only partially known, and are known differently by different individuals; that in human beings contradictions are more normal than logical consistencies; and that the Gospels did not purport to be documented histories such as we demand today. As one broods over the records and lives in imagination with the apostles, they take on flesh and blood. But genuine acquaintance demands more than brooding; it necessitates real effort, immensely rewarded with excellent companionship. Beyond companionship with the apostles is the further reward of a new appreciation of their Lord.

There are three sources of information on the apostles, of which the New Testament is the most important. Although it does not give all the information desired, it is none the less the most valuable and trustworthy resource for understanding the Twelve.

Tradition is a second source of insight. In the past Roman

Catholics have used tradition more extensively than Protestants. At the time of the Reformation miracle-working bones and artifacts were scattered all over Europe and the stories attached to the relics were as marvelous as the cures they wrought. These fanciful tales, little better than fairy stories parading under the cloak of religion, so alienated the enlightened mind of the Renaissance that religious folklore lost most of its value.

Out of this vast morass of folk stories, two types are of help for a better understanding of the apostles. One augments the scriptural material with illustrations of characteristics of the apostles, for example, the stories of the aged apostle John converting a robber, and of Peter returning to Rome. The other comprises living tradition—tradition accepted in whole or in part by large numbers of modern Christians. Illustrative of these traditions are the stories of Andrew as he relates to Scotland, James to Spain, and Thomas to India.

A third source of information that throws light upon the lives of the apostles is historical writing outside the New Testament. Unfortunately we have little Christian literature that was written during the first century, but there is abundant information from non-Christian sources which describes conditions during the apostolic period. A study of the land, the people, and the events of the first century helps toward an appreciation of the manner of life and the kind of problems which confronted the apostles in the world of that time.

That Jesus placed great importance on the selection of the Twelve from among the larger group of disciples is evident from a study of his life pattern. He prepared for every major decision by a period of prayer. Before beginning his public ministry he spent forty days in meditation and prayer; he spent a night in prayer before his Transfiguration and a night in prayer before his Crucifixion. Likewise he spent the night in prayer before choosing the Twelve.

What task did he envision for this group that made their choice such a major decision? Mark gives two reasons for the appointment of the Twelve. First, they were "to be with him." The Twelve who were "with him" helped our Lord face human nature as it is. It is not too difficult to plan an ideal social order if all we deal with is the imagination. Plato created an ideal republic, Thomas More, a utopia; Bacon, a new Atlantis; H. G. Wells, new worlds for old. Jesus also set forth an ideal social order, the Kingdom of God. But while the great minds who built republics and utopias and new worlds used pen and paper, Jesus established his Kingdom of God with living people. He embodied his ideas in a fellowship, a firsthand task that compelled him to keep his feet on the ground. The Twelve were "with him" in this venture and a very human group they were. They interrupted his prayers by their stupidity; they delayed his plans by their personal ambitions; they disturbed his greatest discourses by petty quarrels and bickering. Jesus could close his eyes and be in the presence of God, but as soon as he opened them he looked upon the frailties of his fellow workers. This contact invested his Kingdom of God with vitality and challenge. In today's terminology Jesus needed the Twelve in his laboratory of human relations.

Being himself a human being, Jesus needed fellowship. No man can develop his highest capacity alone; he has to have the action and reaction of his fellows. Nevertheless, great leaders are the loneliest men. Harry Truman, when he was expressing what all men of large responsibility feel, said of his job as President of the United States, "This is a lonely job. Everybody who comes to see me wants me to do something for him. No one comes to me for fellowship." It is this loneliness that leads the president of a company to have an extended conversation with a junior executive, the bishop to prolong the interview with a seminary student, and the author to chat with the cab driver. Jesus shared the loneliness that is the price of leadership.

Although most of Jesus' public ministry was spent under the pressure of crowds, the throngs could not satisfy his need for close fellowship. When the going was difficult and the crowds began to leave, his loneliness expressed itself in a question to his disciples, "Will you also go away?" How glad he must have been when Peter replied, "Lord, to whom shall we go? You have the words of eternal life."

Jesus took his disciples "with him" to the Garden of Gethsemane. As in agony he sweated, God sent angels to comfort him, but even the angels could not meet Jesus' need for human fellowship. When heavy with weariness the disciples slept, he awoke them, asking, "Could you not watch with me one hour?"

Jesus' second reason for choosing the Twelve was that they might "be sent out to preach, and have authority to cast out demons." Obviously, Jesus himself was limited to one place and one time. He could not do all the good that needed to be done; so he chose the Twelve to augment his effectiveness. In sending them forth he was multiplying his own power.

No doubt he was also thinking of someone to carry on his work after his death. Scholars variously estimate the length of Jesus' public ministry between six months and three years. Moreover, long or short, his public ministry was carried on in the shadow of a cross. At death, had he not left behind him some followers who had caught his spirit, his Gospel would have been sealed in the tomb with his body. After he arose he was seen only by those who had believed; the Twelve who had been "with him" and had been "sent forth" by him were the ones through whom the Lord carried on his work.

No one lives in this world beyond his lifetime except as he lives in others. George Whitefield was perhaps the greatest preacher of the eighteenth century. John Wesley, though not as great a preacher as Whitefield, knew how to prepare other men to preach. He organized classes with leaders; he set up societies and appointed local preachers. Whitefield was an orator; Wesley was a leader. Whitefield left a memory; Wesley left a church. The prophets of the Old Testament and the orders of the Roman Catholic Church illustrate the same truth.

In view of the magnitude of the task to be entrusted to these

Twelve, their calls appear unspectacular. Luke tells the story in this wise, "He went out into the hills to pray; and all night he continued in prayer to God. And when it was day, he called his disciples, and chose from them Twelve, whom he named apostles."

Not one of the Twelve refused his call. Each one came gladly to follow the Master. For some this call meant leaving father and mother, brother and sister, wife and child. One left a lucrative seat of customs; some laid aside their nets. To all the enlistment meant forsaking the security of home for the adversities of a traveling man of God; for most it meant a martyr's death. But as Jesus later reminded them, no one left family, houses, or land without receiving a hundredfold more in this world and in the world to come life everlasting.

Peter left his nets but his faith became the rock on which the Church of Jesus Christ was built. Matthew left his gold but affixed his name to the first book of the New Testament. John left his boat but became "the beloved disciple" whose words are graven on the heart of every lover of our Lord. With the exception of Judas there was not a disciple who did not become larger of mind and bigger of spirit because he was with the Master. They knew higher joy and deeper sorrows in his fellowship, and thus fulfilled his promise of abundant life. Is there any group of men in all human history more worth knowing than the Twelve whom Jesus chose to be with him?

2

Simon Peter, World-Wide Fisherman

ST. PETER'S DAY June 29

The Collect

O Almighty God, who by thy Son Jesus Christ didst give to thy Apostle Saint Peter many excellent gifts, and commandedst him earnestly to feed thy flock; Make, we beseech thee, all Bishops and Pastors diligently to preach thy holy Word, and the people obediently to follow the same, that they may receive the crown of everlasting glory; through the same thy Son Jesus Christ our Lord. *Amen.*

DEPART FROM ME, FOR I AM A SINFUL MAN, O LORD," Simon exclaimed as he fell down and clasped the knees of Jesus. A seaside sermon followed by a miraculous catch of fish had shown Simon his weakness and his need. Because he realized his unworthiness, he begged Jesus to depart from him. But Jesus understood the confused emotions that caused Simon to contradict his words by his actions —to clasp Jesus' knees even while urging him to leave—and he calmed Simon's fears, promising that in the future he would catch men, not fish. The record states simply that Simon "left everything and followed him."

Sometime later a violent storm at midnight tossed the boat in which the disciples were crossing the Sea of Galilee. They were in great fear when Jesus appeared, walking on the water, and said, "It is I; have no fear." Simon called out, "Lord, if it is you, bid me come to you on the water." As long as his eye was fixed on Jesus, he walked successfully; but when he looked at the waves and realized the strength of the wind, he felt a sudden uprush of fear and began to sink. "Lord, save me," he cried. Jesus took his hand and said, "O man of little faith, why did you doubt?"

In the first of these incidents James and John were with Simon and in the second all the apostles were present. It was Simon, however, who fell down to clasp the knees of Jesus. It was Simon who walked on the water, sank, and was saved. It was Simon who said, "Depart from me," "Bid me come to you." As far as the record goes little would be lost if the other apostles were absent, but all the story would be lost without Simon.

In these brief episodes Simon was brave and cowardly, wise and foolish, accepting and rejecting, fearless and fearful, a man of doubt and a man of faith. He was an uninhibited, impulsive man who talked and acted before he thought. If these observations rested on two simple stories only, they would properly be questioned as finding too much in too little. However, the very ample record of Simon found in the New Testament establishes his nature. Simon was constant in his changeableness. Strangely enough, to this man Jesus gave the name Rock (Peter). Why did He choose such a contradictory name for this disciple?

In the latter part of Jesus' ministry he called the disciples to him in Caesarea Philippi and questioned them, "Who do men say that the Son of man is?" They replied, "Some say John the Baptist, others say Elijah, and others Jeremiah or one of the prophets." Jesus then pressed on to the really important question, "Who do you say that I am?" Simon replied, "You are the

Christ, the Son of the living God." According to the first three Gospels, this was the first time that open public confession was made of Jesus as the Christ. Jesus "strictly charged them to tell no one that he was the Christ." Commending Simon for his insight, Jesus said, "Blessed are you Simon Bar-Jona . . . I tell you, you are a rock (Petra) and on this rock (Petra) I will build my church." Henceforth Simon was known as Peter. In the Fourth Gospel John indicates that this name was given at the call of Simon to discipleship. Mark records the name as given at the time of the call to apostleship. Matthew has the time correspond with the Great Confession. Whatever the exact time of Simon's renaming, the meaning was made clear when he made the Great Confession.

On this occasion there was an exchange of names. Peter called Jesus "the Christ," the name by which his followers henceforth knew him; and in calling Simon "Peter," Jesus created a name which many men have since proudly borne. Immediately following this interchange Jesus declared, "I will give you the keys of the kingdom of heaven and whatever you bind on earth shall be bound in heaven, and whatever you loose on earth shall be loosed in heaven." This word of praise has become the subject of sharp controversy. The Roman Catholics contend that Jesus' reference to the keys of the kingdom of heaven indicate that Peter and the popes who inherit Peter's authority have the key to man's eternal destiny. Protestants turn away from the concept of vested authority over man's destiny on earth and in heaven and stress Peter's *faith* in "Christ, the Son of the living God" as the foundation of their religion. Deep as is the gulf which these interpretations place between Protestants and Catholics, both sincerely unite in the praise given Simon by our Lord, "Blessed are you Simon Bar-Jona! For flesh and blood have not revealed this to you, but my Father who is in heaven."

Few of the characteristics of a rock appear in the Gospel stories about Peter. A rock is firmly set, solid, immovable, silent; Simon Peter shifted easily and was never silent. "Lord, how often shall my brother sin against me, and I forgive him?" "Lord, are you telling this parable for us or for all?" "Lo, we have left everything, and followed you." "Explain the parable to us." "Master, look! The fig tree which you cursed has withered." On and on he goes. If any one of the Twelve speaks, it is more than an even chance that Peter will be the one.

On the Mount of Transfiguration, thrilled at the sight of Jesus with Moses and Elijah but embarrassed by the silence of the holy moment, Peter burst out, "Let us make three booths, one for you one for Moses one for Elijah." A foolish thing to say. Who but Peter would talk about rushing around for branches to build booths when he stood in the presence of immortals? The Gospel writer excuses Peter by adding, "He did not know what to say." Like many who have come after him, not knowing what to say did not keep Peter's mouth shut. Although his words frequently got him into trouble, Peter never learned to be silent. Chrysostom, three centuries later, called him "the mouthpiece of the disciples."

Moreover, mere talk did not satisfy Peter. He was always doing something. He fell down to clasp Jesus' knees, walked on the sea, wanted to build tabernacles for Moses, Elijah, and Jesus. When Peter and John ran to the tomb to verify the Resurrection of Jesus, John, the younger, arrived first at the tomb, but impetuous Peter rushed into it first. On one occasion after the Resurrection the disciples were fishing in Lake Galilee when Jesus became dimly visible in the early dawn. John with his intuitive insight exclaimed, "It is the Lord!" Peter with characteristic impulsiveness threw aside his cloak and swam ashore. The others could row ashore but Peter must rush to his Master.

In Gethsemane Jesus, aware of the approaching crisis, sought strength in fellowship and prayer, in which Peter, James, and John were especially asked to join. But the strain of the day and the quiet of the night were too much for Peter. He fell asleep. To be sure, he was not the first or the last of the saints to slumber over his prayers or to nod in the presence of the Lord. When the clash of armor and the flare of torches aroused him and he realized that Jesus was in danger, he drew his sword and "struck the High Priest's slave and cut off his right ear." It was a foolish thing to do. But once Peter was awake the enemies of the Lord had better look after their ears, for he was quick with his sword. Jesus showed his disapproval by promptly healing the wounded servant's ear. Peter's impetuous disposition was never entirely changed. He was always going into action—wise or foolish.

The uninhibited person, who speaks and acts impulsively, guided more by feeling than by thought, is always capable of great heights of exaltation and great depths of despair. Modern psychology calls this range of response "mood swing," but the old-fashioned words "uprising and downcasting" are more vivid. What rare experiences of uprising and downcasting Simon Peter attained!

How exalted Peter must have been when Jesus said to him, "Blessed are you Simon Bar-Jona! For flesh and blood have not revealed this to you but my Father which is in heaven." Mortal man has never received higher praise than this tribute paid to Peter by Jesus Christ. Immediately afterward, Jesus explained to his disciples that he must go to Jerusalem and suffer many things and be killed. Scandalized, Peter exclaimed, "God forbid, Lord! This shall never happen to you." Jesus, whose heart was set on the will of the Father, recognized this instinctive appeal to the will to live as the voice of Satan. He turned upon Peter and severely rebuked him, "Get behind me, Satan! You are a hindrance to me; for you are not on the side of God, but of men." Thus, in a matter of moments, Peter had been commended as God-inspired and condemned as Satan, a hindrance to his Master. What uprising and downcasting!

Peter appears again in the incident of Jesus washing the disciples' feet. Luke says that on this last night, "a dispute also arose among them, which of them was to be regarded as the greatest." There is reason to believe that this dispute was between

Peter and Judas over the honor of sitting at the Lord's left hand. Jesus rebuked this seeking of "Lordship" and held up to highest honor "one who serves." Immediately, Peter, taking the words of Jesus in full seriousness, went from the head of the table to the very last place. He would be first in humility if he was not first in honor.

Jesus then followed his verbal teaching by a demonstration of humility. "Jesus, knowing . . . that he had come from God and was going to God, rose from supper, laid aside his garments, and girded himself with a towel. Then he poured water into a basin, and began to wash the disciples' feet." He began at the head of the table and washed all their feet until he came to Peter, now bowed in humility at the end of the table. "You shall never wash my feet," Peter protested. Jesus replied, "If I do not wash you, you have no part in me." Whereupon Peter quickly swung to the opposite extreme, "Lord, not only my feet but also my hands and my head." How like Peter! First in honor or first in humility, not a drop of water or a full bath. What downcasting and uprising!

On the last night of Jesus' earthly life he said, "You will all fall away because of me this night." Peter protested, "Though they all fall away because of you, I will never fall away." Jesus replied, "This very night, before the cock crows, you will deny me three times." Peter declared, "Even if I must die with you, I will not deny you."

But the confident faith of the upper room faded in the outer court of the High Priest. Under the insistent questioning of a servant girl Peter thrice denied his Lord, declaring with oaths, "I do not know the man!" At this point Jesus turned and looked at him. That one look brought to Peter's mind his boast of faithfulness. Stricken with remorse, "he went out and wept bitterly." What an overwhelming experience of uprising and downcasting.

Information on Peter comes from all four Gospels. Mark, the first Gospel written, was undoubtedly used by the other writers, especially by Matthew and Luke. Tradition declares that Peter was the source of Mark's information. It is significant that, except for his attempt to walk on the water, the Gospel of Mark contains all the unfavorable information about Peter contained in the other Gospels. Had Peter seen fit to omit these unfavorable reports, or had he retold them in a more favorable light, the entire impression of his character would be changed.

Luke and John do not mention the rebuke of Jesus, "Get behind me, Satan." Mark and Matthew record it. Luke says Jesus rebuked *all* the disciples for sleeping while he prayed; Mark says Jesus rebuked Peter only and Matthew again uses the words of Mark. Luke and Paul say that the risen Lord appeared first to Peter. Mark does not record any Resurrection appearance to Peter. Why the omission? If it was Peter who told his story to Mark, he usually told the entire story. Moreover, if there was any shading to be done, he let it be against him, not in his favor. Peter rose at times to greatness.

Peter not only admitted his faults; he accepted the deserved rebuke. Benedict Arnold, whose name spells treason to every American, betrayed his country after George Washington mildly rebuked him for two trivial offenses of which he was proved guilty. But Peter could take severe rebuke. His loyalty was unshaken when Jesus said, "Get behind me, Satan." The look Jesus gave him at the time of his denial brought tears of remorse, but no resentment. Beside Lake Galilee the resurrected Lord thrice questioned him, "Do you love me?" In spite of having to affirm his love before his fellow apostles not once or twice but three times, Peter took the inquiry in the spirit of love in which it was given. Evidently he knew his own weaknesses, so he was set free from resentment and was able to take rebuke to his soul's betterment.

These qualities of Peter make him live after nineteen centuries. While discussing some of the facets of Peter's nature, a teacher of a church-school adult class was interrupted by a woman who excitedly exclaimed, "I like Peter best of all!" Well she might, for she was much like him. In fact, so many of us are like Peter that he is very generally loved. His blunders, his inconsistencies, his foolish words, and his senseless acts serve only to draw us closer to his side.

With all his weaknesses how could Jesus have characterized Peter as the Rock? Because beneath his changeableness was a firmness of loyalty and conviction that remained unshaken. His faith and love were the spiritual foundation that Jesus sensed when he gave Simon his new name. Peter's faith found expression in the Great Confession which he never recanted. His love was indicated in his final reply to Jesus' thrice-repeated question, "Lord, you know everything; you know that I love you." Peter may not always have lived up to his protestations, but there is no indication of any wavering in his love for Jesus, Son of God. On this foundation of unshaken faith and love rests the Church of Jesus Christ. The gates of hell shall not prevail against it.

Peter, leader of the apostles during Jesus' life, remained the acknowledged leader of the early Christian Church. He was central in the story of the early Church even as he was central in the Gospel story. When the apostle James was beheaded Peter fled from Jerusalem for safety, and James, the brother of our Lord, took Peter's place as leader of the Jerusalem church. After the apostles gathered for the Council of Jerusalem, Peter disappears from the biblical record.

What kind of church leader was Peter? Church leaders are usually selected for maturity of judgment and balance of mind. Now and then a leader is selected because he is an able preacher, a skillful organizer, a dynamic promoter, or simply because he is a good fellow whom everybody likes. Would a responsible church body elect a man like Simon Peter head of a church? He would appear more likely to blow up than to build up the church.

What happened to Simon Peter so that he was "reputed to be a pillar" of the church? Did he remain the impetuous, constant-in-changeableness Simon Peter of the Gospel record? Not quite. There were signs of similarity, but evidently he developed a strength and stability that were not apparent in the Gospel record.

In the early church Peter was "the mouthpiece of the disciples" as he had been during Jesus' lifetime. Six of his speeches are recorded in the Acts of the Apostles. The first and greatest is the famous sermon on the day of Pentecost. This sermon, accompanied by overwhelming manifestation of the Spirit, was responsible for the conversion of 3,000 souls. In view of the number of people affected, the wide area from which they came, and the effect upon the future of the Christian Church, no other sermon in the long history of Christianity has produced such tremendous results. The birth of the Christian Church is properly dated from Peter's sermon.

The record also preserves Peter's address to the crowd at Solomon's Portico near the Beautiful Gate of the Temple, his defense before the scribes and elders, his speech to Cornelius, his report of Cornelius' conversion to the church at Jerusalem, and his address to the Jerusalem Council in justification of taking the Gospel to the Gentiles. This is considerable discourse when the condensed form of the record in the Acts of the Apostles is taken into account. Nor are these speeches trivial or self-contradictory, as was much of Peter's talk in the earlier days. They represent balanced judgment combined with evangelistic fervor and zeal. They do honor to him and to the Christian Church.

In the early Church Peter remained a man of action as well as a man of words. He preached, he healed the sick, he carried the Gospel to distant places, he was twice imprisoned, he was beaten, he officiated on investigating committees, and he disciplined the erring members of the Church. In action, as in speech, Peter was for the most part a vigorous, consistent, and courageous leader.

However, in spite of his achievements, it is not surprising to find signs of his old impetuous nature occasionally showing up in ill-considered word or deed. Several days intervened between the last appearance of the resurrected Christ and the pouring out of the Holy Spirit. Days of inactivity and waiting are hard on men like Simon Peter. Thinking that some use should be made of this time, Peter proposed that the group elect someone to take the place of Judas, whose life had come to a tragic end. The election resulted in the selection of Matthias, an apostle whose name is not mentioned in the New Testament apart from this event. Peter may have been premature in urging this election. It has indications of man's selection rather than God's direction. If Peter could have waited, God might have made his choice manifest as he did when he laid hands on Paul. But waiting was one thing Peter could not endure. He had to speak out and to act.

That Peter never entirely overcame his tendency to fluctuate is indicated in the reversal of his position in regard to eating with the Gentiles. Paul says, "before certain men came from James he [Peter] ate with the Gentiles; but when they came he drew back and separated himself, fearing the circumcision party." The pressure of the strict Jewish sect within the Christian Church was so intense that Peter's reversal is very understandable. Sympathy goes out to the well-meaning apostle caught between desire for fellowship with Gentile Christians and the legal demands of the leaders of the Jerusalem church. Paul, who could not endure wavering or inconsistency, "opposed him to his face, because he stood condemned." It was a difficult situation for all involved.

However, in spite of Paul's open condemnation the two men remained close comrades. The Council of Jerusalem, which dealt with this problem, ended in mutual friendship and good will. Peter retained his admirable ability to admit fault and to take rebuke. The history of Christianity would be brighter if the same could be said of all Christians through the centuries.

Peter also played a vital part in fostering the growth of Christianity from a Jewish sect to a world-wide religion. The 120 followers upon whom the Holy Spirit fell at the day of Pentecost as well as the 3,000 converted on that day were all Jews. It was not until the martyrdom of Stephen scattered the Christians that "Philip [the evangelist, not the apostle] went down to a city of Samaria, and proclaimed to them the Christ." We do not know what human reasoning led Philip to preach to the Samaritans. He knew that the Samaritans were hated as a mixed race, half Jew, half Gentile; that they accepted only the five books of Moses and worshiped in their hills rather than in Jerusalem. The antagonism between Jew and Gentile, which had four centuries of bitterness back of it, he fully understood. Yet Philip, led by God, preached to these people with such power that "unclean spirits came out of many who were possessed. Many who were paralyzed or lame were healed," and much joy came to that city. When word reached Jerusalem of the power of God among the Samaritans, Peter and John were sent to investigate. Arriving in Samaria, they "prayed for them . . . laid their hands on them and they received the Holy Spirit." This gift of the Holy Spirit was an unmistakable sign of God's approval. Peter then knew that God included Samaritans as well as Jews in the Christian fellowship.

The next step in Peter's growing appreciation of the Gentiles was the conversion of Cornelius. The Samaritans were at least half Jews; they believed and obeyed the Mosaic law. But Cornelius was a Roman, a centurian in the Italian cohort. True, he was "a devout man who feared God . . . gave alms liberally to the people, and prayed constantly to God," but he possessed no Jewish blood. One day when Cornelius was at prayer he saw a vision and was told to send for one Simon called Peter who would bring an answer to his prayers.

At the very same time Peter also had a vision. He saw the heavens open and something like a sheet descend, let down by the four corners. In the sheet were all kinds of animals, reptiles, and wild birds. A voice said to him, "Rise, Peter, kill and eat." Peter replied, "No, Lord; for I have never eaten anything that is common or unclean." Then the voice answered, "What God has cleansed you must not call common." Three times the vision was repeated, then it disappeared into heaven.

Immediately, before the vision could vanish from his mind, messengers came from Cornelius requesting Peter to call upon him. Peter responded and when he came to Cornelius' home both men realized that they had been brought together at the call of God. Peter then told Cornelius, his kinsmen, and his close friends about Jesus Christ and the gift of the Holy Spirit. As he spoke, the Holy Spirit fell on all who heard the word, whereupon Peter asked his Christian companions, "Can anyone forbid water for baptizing these people who have received the Holy Spirit just as we have?" The answer was so obvious that they were baptized at once.

On his return to Jerusalem, when he was called to account for his unorthodox behavior in going to uncircumcised men, Peter justified his action on the basis of his heavenly vision attested by the gift of the Holy Spirit. Common sense prevailed and his hearers "glorified God, saying, 'then to the Gentiles also God hath granted repentance unto life.' "

The conversion of Cornelius did more than add a new member to the Christian fellowship. It added new dimension to the Christian message. Peter summarized the new insight when he said, We now know "that God shows no partiality, but in every nation anyone who fears him and does what is right is acceptable to him." This statement, one of the earliest and clearest expressions of the universality of the Gospel message, marked a big step forward in the growth of Christianity toward a world religion.

Since Peter's baptism of Cornelius had established the principle that Gentiles could become Christians, the church at Antioch sent Paul and Barnabas on a long missionary journey, on which they were to make a special effort to win Gentiles to Christianity. In spite of opposition they were greatly encouraged by the results, for they found the Gentiles who had been converted to Judaism far more receptive to the Gospel than the Jews. Returning to Antioch, they reported with enthusiasm that God "had opened a door of faith to the Gentiles."

All was well until some Christians came up from Jerusalem and declared that unless these Gentiles were "circumcised according to the custom of Moses," they could not be saved. After "no small dissension" Paul and Barnabas were appointed a committee to go to Jesusalem to settle the dispute.

The Jerusalem meeting was the first Christian Council. There have been many councils since that time, but none more important. The issue before the council was: Does a Gentile have to become a Jew and subject himself to all the ceremonial and ritual regulations of Moses before he can become a Christian? The total attitude of Christianity toward its Old Testament heritage, as well as toward evangelizing the Gentile world, was involved. The answer to this problem determined whether Christianity would become a Jewish sect or a world religion.

Peter was present with the apostles and elders who "were gathered together to consider this matter." The debate continued for several days. Characteristically, the first recorded speech was by Peter. God has "made no distinction between us and them, but cleansed their hearts by faith," he declared. "Why do you make trial of God by putting a yoke upon the neck of the disciples which neither our fathers nor we have been able to bear? . . . We shall be saved through the grace of the Lord Jesus, just as they will." James concurred in Peter's sentiment.

Finally a formal agreement was written welcoming converted Gentiles into the Christian fellowship on condition that they would abstain from meat offered to idols, from blood and what is strangled, and from unchastity. Thus the problem was settled at the top level. From then on Christianity became a world religion. Although sounds of the controversy echo down the pages of the New Testament, the important decision had been made and in spite of conflict the Christian Gospel became universal in its appeal.

Paul's account of this controversy in his letter to the Galatians indicates that Peter did not arrive at his understanding of the Gentiles' place in the Christian Church without struggle. There is disagreement among scholars on the time sequence of some of the events in this narrative; but whatever the time relation, Peter's struggle is clear. Be it said to the glory of the apostles that throughout all the controversy friendship survived.

Nineteen hundred years have passed since Peter discovered that "God shows no partiality, but in every nation anyone who fears him and does what is right is acceptable to him." Few are the Christians today who would take exception to the principle that God's love and salvation are universal; but practice runs far behind belief.

Peter not only talked and acted, but some scholars believe that he was an author and credit him with writing I Peter, although not II Peter. Many of the ideas sound like Peter's. Who better than he could warn "to keep the tongue from evil," to live "no longer by human passions but by the will of God," and to resist "your adversary the devil"? For half a chapter Peter, enlarging upon the play of words on his name, "the Rock," speaks about "living stones." He enjoins Christians to become like their Master, "stones . . . built into a spiritual house—holy—acceptable to God through Jesus Christ." Stones can be used for building, but, Peter warned, they can also "make men stumble." Look therefore to God "who called you out of darkness into his marvelous light," and be grateful that from him you have "received mercy." These are injunctions that a man like Peter could give, for they grew out of his own experience.

Peter's claim to literary fame rests more firmly on his relation to the Gospel of Mark. Papias of Hierapolis recorded the fact that "Mark, the interpreter of Peter, wrote down carefully what he remembered, both the sayings and the deeds of Christ, but not in chronological order, for he did not hear the Lord and he did not accompany him. At a later time, however, he did accompany Peter, who adapted his instruction to the needs [of his hearers], but not with the object of making a connected series of discourses of our Lord. So Mark made no mistake in writing the individual discourses in the order in which he recalled them."

On this authority it is believed that Mark served as translator for Peter when he preached in Rome. As Peter told and retold his experiences with Jesus, Mark interpreted them again and again to Christian groups. This frequent repetition gave Mark an almost verbatim memory of Peter's recollections. After the death of Peter, Mark, realizing the value of Peter's firsthand account, recorded what he remembered so clearly in the document we know as the first of the Gospel records. Matthew and Luke obviously used Mark's Gospel in the writing of their lives of Jesus. In this manner Peter became the source for our earliest Gospel and thus to a large extent supplied the material for the first written record of our Lord. If this reconstruction of events is accurate, Mark's Gospel can be considered Peter's personal remembrance of his life with Jesus. As such it remains one of Peter's greatest contributions to the Christian Church.

The end of Peter's life is lost in mystery. After the Council of Jerusalem his name disappears from the Acts of the Apostles. Clement of Rome, writing his First Epistle in 96 A.D., said that Peter "after having thus borne testimony went to his well deserved place of glory," later adding that he "joined a great multitude of the elect, who . . . suffered many outrages because of jealousy and became a shining example among us." The last two words "among us," are taken to mean Rome and to signify that Peter suffered martyrdom there along with other followers of the faith. Although Clement of Rome is one of the earliest Christian writers, apart from the authors of the New Testament itself, and thus becomes a valuable source of information, unfortunately his testimony about Peter in Rome is indirect and subject to more than one interpretation. None the less, added to other traditions of later date, it has caused many scholars to believe that Peter preached Christ in Rome and suffered martyrdom there.

It is deduced that Peter died in Rome at the time of the persecution of the Christians by Nero. During this persecution, tradition says, the Christians prevailed upon Peter to flee for his life. Against his own desire he yielded to his friends and fled down the Appian Way, but as he was leaving the city he saw a vision of his Master going toward Rome. Falling before him, Peter inquired, *"Quo vadis, Domine?"* (Where are you going, Master?) Jesus replied, "To Rome to be crucified anew." Peter turned back to the city and when condemned to death by crucifixion made the request that he be crucified head downward because he was not worthy to die as had his Lord. In death as in life he preserved the characteristics that endear him to Christians everywhere.

Two traditional burial places exist for Peter: one under the Cathedral of Saint Peter on Vatican Hill, the other in the catacombs of the Basilica of Saint Sebastian on the Appian Way. It has not as yet been established which, if either, has the proper claim.

Chrysostom, who called Peter "the mouthpiece of the disciples," also said he was "the leader of the apostolic chorus—the pillar of the church, the basis of faith, the foundation of our confession, the World-Wide Fisherman who brought our race heavenward from the abyss of error."

Jesus had promised Peter that he would become a fisher of men. In Jerusalem, Samaria, Lydda, Joppa, Caesarea, Pontus, Galatia, Cappodocia, Asia, Bithynia, Antioch, Corinth, and Rome, Peter cast the Gospel net. Indeed, this Galilean fisherman cast his net so wide and so well that he has become the World-Wide Fisherman.

3

Andrew, the Friend

ST. ANDREW'S DAY November 30

The Collect

Almighty God, who didst give such grace unto thy holy Apostle Saint Andrew, that he readily obeyed the calling of thy Son Jesus Christ, and followed him without delay; Grant unto us all, that we, being called by thy holy Word, may forthwith give up ourselves obediently to fulfill thy holy commandments; through the same Jesus Christ our Lord. *Amen.*

ANDREW AND HIS FRIEND STOOD BESIDE THE JORDAN with the prophet John, called the Baptist. It was dusk, and in the distance a stranger was seen approaching. Andrew sensed nothing unusual about the figure, but John gazed at the stranger appraisingly, hushed in sudden silence, as if he were seeing beyond time and person to some eternal meaning. Then breaking the silence, he spoke, but not in the fiery tone of his usual pronouncements. Rather he spoke in a half whisper as if his thoughts found utterance without volition on his part. "Behold," he said, "the Lamb of God."

Before he reached the three men, the stranger turned in the

direction of a larger group. Andrew and his friend quietly followed the stranger, and so absorbed was John in his insight that he did not appear to know they had left until they disappeared from view.

John the Baptist was not surprised, and certainly not disappointed, when Andrew and his friend left him. He considered himself only "the voice of one crying in the wilderness." He saw himself only as one preparing the way of the Lord, making his paths straight. His message was, "Repent, for the kingdom of heaven is at hand." Multitudes had flocked to hear him, for his was the first prophetic voice heard in Israel for four hundred years, but he expected men to turn from him to a greater Voice who was to come.

Andrew, along with others who had responded to John's message, had already been baptized in the Jordan. As he had come from the water he had felt his soul washed clean, and this sense of cleansing intensified his longing for the next step, finding the greater one who would reveal "the salvation of God." Thus when John the Baptist said of the stranger, "Behold, the Lamb of God," Andrew realized that the object of his longing had appeared before him.

This stranger whom John the Baptist had called the Lamb of God saw Andrew and his friend approaching and asked, "What do you seek?" Unwilling to disclose their motives so soon but too excited to restrain their eagerness, they replied, "Teacher, where are you staying?" When the stranger invited them to "come and see," they accepted the invitation and stayed with him until sunrise the next day. Probably they were part of a group who talked the night through. As dawn came it was a new day in a double sense for Andrew, for he now knew that this man called Jesus of Nazareth was, as John had discerned, the Lamb of God, the Saviour of the world.

Emotion swept over him in the wake of his discovery that here was the Messiah. The cleansing of baptism unto repentance, great as that experience had been, did not compare with the elevation of spirit which rose with discovery of the Lamb of

God. However, great emotional experiences are usually followed by periods of depression unless some appropriate expression of the emotion immediately follows the spiritual uplift.

Andrew did not reason about his experience, but, following the prompting of his own spirit, he retained his elevation of soul by communicating it to another. He went to find his own brother, Simon, and in great excitement said, "We have found the Messiah." Simon was naturally incredulous, so Andrew brought him to Jesus, to let him judge the truth of the discovery for himself. This incident, described in the first chapter of John's Gospel, makes Andrew the first disciple called by our Lord and the first to bring another disciple to Jesus. If his total recorded achievements are compared with those of his brother Simon Peter, he was one of the less prominent apostles. Peter is a towering personality, a natural leader whose words and acts stand out on almost every page of the Gospels and the first fifteen chapters of Acts. In contrast, knowledge about Andrew is limited to a few brief passages. Yet Andrew brought Peter to Christ and, by his bringing, shares in the honor that belongs to Peter as leader of the Twelve.

Fortunately, John's Gospel also gives us two other incidents that clothe Andrew with personality. On one occasion, when Jesus and his disciples wanted to get away from the press of the crowd, they crossed over the Sea of Galilee. But the people would not be so easily dismissed and they walked around the lake; before long the throng around Jesus was as great as ever. It was an exciting time with the healing of the sick and the parry and thrust of pointed discussion. The hours sped and evening approached with the crowd far from home and without food. Jesus asked, "How are we to buy bread so that these people may eat?" Philip answered, "Two hundred denarii would not buy enough bread for each of them to get a little." Then Andrew, who had evidently been searching for food, came forward with a boy and said, "There is a lad here who has five barley loaves and two fish; but what are they among so many?" Jesus called the boy to him, took the loaves, gave thanks to God, and began to distribute the food to the people. In the hands of Jesus the small lunch was sufficient for the entire multitude.

In this story Andrew is again bringing someone to Jesus. This time it is not a future disciple but a boy with his picnic lunch. Probably Andrew had no idea of the miracle about to be performed when he brought the lad with his loaves to Jesus. Yet he realized that at that moment a boy with the needed food, even in a small amount, was of interest and importance to Jesus, so he brought the boy to the Master.

Edward Kimball, a successful merchant in Boston, once saw a young man selling shoes in a small shop. The young man, like many others in every large city, had come from the country, and was poor, without family, friends, or funds. Mr. Kimball was drawn to him and took him to his Sunday school. Soon the country boy was soundly converted and in turn began teaching Sunday school. He moved from Boston to Chicago and took on still larger leadership. Finally he abandoned business for Christian work and became the greatest evangelist of his day, Dwight L. Moody. Edward Kimball, who brought Moody to Christ, was another Andrew.

The final story about Andrew occurs during the last week of our Lord's earthly life. Some Greeks came to the Feast of the Passover. Everywhere they heard wonderful reports about the prophet, Jesus of Nazareth, and they wanted to know the man so widely talked about. Since they were Greeks and strangers to many customs of the Jews, these worshipers sought help from Philip, whose Greek name attracted their attention. "Sir," they said to Philip, "we wish to see Jesus." Philip introduced the genial Andrew and together they brought the Greeks to Jesus. Moved by the Gentiles' desire to see him, Jesus opened his heart and talked to them about life and death, suffering and salvation. There is no record to indicate how much of Jesus' talk they understood, or whether they followed the events of the next few days to their culmination in the Cross and the open tomb. Whatever their response, the Greeks, by Andrew's help, met the Master and heard the Gospel from his lips.

Andrew's evangelism always seemed to be based on personal friendship. He brought others to Jesus because he himself was a friend of Jesus. With Andrew it was love at first sight, at last sight, and at every sight in between. There is no record of any vacillation or coldness in Andrew's friendship with Jesus. From the time that John pointed out the Lamb of God until Jesus disappeared into heaven, Andrew was the loyal follower. Nothing in Andrew's life was as important as this transforming friendship.

In John's Gospel are found all the references to Andrew that give him individuality. Thus the conjecture that Andrew was an especial friend of the author of the Fourth Gospel is strengthened. If any of this Gospel is the work of John, son of Zebedee, the friendship becomes very obvious, for Peter and Andrew, James and John, were partners as fishermen.

A portion of a very ancient copy of the New Testament, preserved by Muratori, indicates that Andrew had some part in the writing of the Gospel of John. "The Fourth Gospel [was written] by John, one of the Twelve," the ancient document says. "When his fellow disciples and bishops urgently pressed him he said, 'Fast with me (from) today, for three days, and let us tell one another any revelation which may be made to us, either for or against (the plan of writing)!' On the same night it was revealed to Andrew, one of the apostles, that John should relate all in his own name, and that all should review (his writings)." This information, which might not withstand critical examination, is none the less of interest in the joining together of the names of John and Andrew. By tradition Andrew has been an especial friend of John's.

Although Andrew appears to have been completely overshadowed by his brother Simon, there was never any hint of jealousy or antagonism. The twelve apostles are always listed in Scripture as "first, Simon, who is called Peter, and Andrew his brother." No one likes to be constantly referred to as "so-and-so's brother," but to be crowded off the pages of Scripture is even worse. If Andrew had known how the New Testament was to take form he might have asked why the four Gospels and the first twelve chapters of Acts devoted to Peter 60 per cent of the lines given the apostles while his own record was confined to a few brief references in the Gospel of John, but he seems to have been concerned only with serving his Master.

In all lists of the Apostles found in the New Testament Peter, Andrew, James, and John are the first four names. As one of this group Andrew could naturally expect to share the common experiences of the others. Yet Peter, James, and John were taken apart by our Lord on several important occasions, such as the healing of Jairus' daughter, the Transfiguration, the Garden of Gethsemane, when Andrew was left out. The grace to accept being left out is an important aspect of friendship. People with chips on their shoulders, looking for slights, seeking intentional or unintentional neglect, can never enjoy true friendship. Andrew was a friend who could be left behind.

Andrew is never mentioned alone in the Gospel records. But then friendly people are seldom found alone; they seek other people and others seek them. So with Andrew.

After the day of Pentecost dependable information about Andrew is not available; his name disappears from the New Testament. But whatever is lacking in solid fact is well supplied by tradition. One of the oldest poems in the English language, perhaps as old as *Beowulf,* is *Andrea.* It records the adventures of Andrew and Matthias in the Land of the Cannibals and the long conversation of Andrew with the angelic boatman who took him on the journey there. While the supposed facts in this story are beyond credence, the early interest in Andrew is significant.

Andrew is said to have carried the Gospel to Russia, Greece, Asia Minor, and Turkey. It was early believed that he lived to a very old age and died a martyr's death on November 30 in the year 69 at Patras in Achaea, Greece. His missionary work in this city, the story goes, was especially successful. Among the many converts was Maximilla, wife of the Roman proconsul Aegeas. Enraged at Andrew's success in the city and in his own household, Aegeas ordered him to lead the people in sacrifice to the heathen gods. Upon his refusal Andrew was severely beaten and then crucified. To make his death the more lingering he was fastened to the cross with cords instead of the customary nails. The cross, shaped like the letter X, is sometimes called the *crux decussata,* but more frequently St. Andrew's cross. As he lingered on the cross for two days he preached to the people, praising God, exhorting his listeners to repentance and faith, and instructing them in the Gospel. After his death, Maximilla, the wife of the proconsul, claimed the body and buried it with loving care in her tomb.

Tradition further recounts that the remains of St. Andrew were afterward removed to Constantinople by Constantine the Great and buried with great solemnity in the magnificent church erected in his honor. His body is said to have remained there until 369, when an abbot named Regulus took portions of it—an armbone, three fingers of the right hand, and three toes—and started on a missionary journey. His journey was long and stormy and at length he was shipwrecked in the county of Fife, Scotland. There Regulus and the few monks who escaped buried again the bones of St. Andrew and built a chapel in his honor. One of the monks converted the Pict king, who erected a new and costly church on the site of the first structure. The place was named St. Andrews and retains that name to this day.

In the eighth century, when Scotland was at war with England, Achaias, King of Scotland, was leading a force of men inferior in equipment and battle position to the English under the leadership of King Athelstan. Indeed, the English outnumbered the Scots three to one. On the night before the battle King Achaias was greatly discouraged as defeat seemed inevitable. After his force had fallen asleep he was wandering over the hillside, surveying his soldiers and trying to arrive at some answer to his difficult problem, when he noticed that the priests who accompanied the Scottish army had erected the St. Andrew's cross on a standard so that it might be a focal point of worship for men facing the dangers of battle. The sight of the cross renewed his faith in his cause and his men and he spent the night making battle plans. Toward dawn he saw, directly over the camp, a large white St. Andrew's cross against the deep blue of the sky, illumined by the first bright shafts of sunrise and glowing with an unearthly beauty. Achaias accepted the vision as a sign from God that St. Andrew would fight for Scotland. He aroused his troops and attacked the enemy with such vigor and courage that the English threw down their arms and fled across the border.

From this time Scotland has used a white cross of St. Andrew on a blue background as its national symbol. When Great Britain adopted a national emblem, the crosses of St. Andrew, St. George, and St. Patrick were combined to form the Union Jack. The flag used by George Washington at Cambridge on January 2, 1776, was constructed of thirteen alternate red and white stripes with the combined crosses of St. Andrew and St. George in the blue canton in place of stars.

In 1411 St. Andrews University, the oldest university in Scotland, was founded on the site on which Regulus first landed. For a long time it offered only theology, but has since expanded its curriculum to include medicine and the arts. St. Andrews University has the distinction of being the place where John Knox first spoke as a preacher of the Reformed Faith in Scotland. Here, too, Patrick Hamilton suffered martyrdom in 1528, as well as John George Wishart in 1546, James Wesby in 1422, and Paul Craco in 1432.

So deeply has St. Andrew woven himself into the traditions, symbols, and affections of Scotland that he appears to belong to the Scots in a special manner. His friendly nature has also appropriately connected him with fraternal organizations. Sons of Scotland take pride in the Scottish Order of St. Andrew and observe November 30, the anniversary of the martyrdom of St. Andrew, as their day of celebration. In the United States the Scottish Order of St. Andrew was for many years active in giving material aid to newly arrived immigrants. Since the need for this service no longer exists, the order has become largely social and concerns itself with colorful Scottish costumes, folk dances, and bagpipe music. The twenty-ninth degree in the ancient and accepted Scottish Rite of Freemasonry is known as the order of "Grand Scottish Knight of St. Andrew," and its primary lessons are Andrew's traits—humility, patience, and self-denial. The Order of the Golden Fleece, instituted in the fifteenth century by Philip the Good, likewise honored St. Andrew as its patron saint and had as its greatest treasure a portion of the wood from St. Andrew's cross. St. Andrew is also the patron saint of fishermen, of Russia (before the Revolution), of Burgundy, and of Hungary.

The simple Gospel portrait of Andrew, the friend, is the basis for an order of young men in the Protestant Episcopal Church. The Brotherhood of St. Andrew is based on the idea of utilizing friendship as a method of bringing young men to Jesus. Each member is expected to strive to bring a friend under the influence of the Gospel, to grasp his hand and place it in the hand of Jesus.

As a chemist uses a catalyst to bring together elements that otherwise will not unite, so a friend brings together people who belong together. The evangelism of friendship recognizes, as Andrew so well knew, that Jesus, not his followers, works the miracles. The drunkard who staggered up to his minister and stammered, "I am one of your converts," received the correct reply, "You appear to be one of *my* converts. When the Lord Jesus converts people, they stay converted." Andrew could not change men but Jesus could. This kind of evangelism, undergirding vast mass movements, motivating house-to-house visitation, or quietly practiced as friend with friend, is the ultimate source of strength and growth for the Christian Gospel.

If the saints in heaven could reach down to our troubled earth, St. Andrew would probably stretch out his hand and say, "Come, my friend, I want you to know my friend, Jesus." What a joy to enter the Master's presence with a hand in the hand of Andrew, the friend!

4 James, the First Apostolic Martyr

ST. JAMES' DAY July 25

The Collect

Grant, O merciful God, that as thine holy Apostle Saint James, leaving his father and all that he had, without delay was obedient unto the calling of thy Son Jesus Christ, and followed him; so we, forsaking all worldly and carnal affections, may be evermore ready to follow thy holy commandments; through the same Jesus Christ our Lord. *Amen.*

JAMES WAS A FISHERMAN TOGETHER WITH HIS BROTHER John, his father Zebedee, and the brothers Peter and Andrew. Bethsaida Julias, probable home of the fishermen, was the fast-growing capital of Ituraea and provided an excellent market for their fish. Should the catch exceed the demands of the local market, Capernaum was easily accessible for the sale of the surplus. If these markets were flooded the fish were salted for sale as far inland as Jerusalem. In a warm climate with slow transportation and no refrigeration, the salting of fish became an important industry. In fact the village of Tarichaea

(Pickle) had grown to some size because of its convenient location a few miles south of Bethsaida (Fishhouse).

James and his partners ran a large-scale enterprise, probably a wholesale business. They fished in deep water, an operation that required sizable boats, heavy nets, and several hands to work the equipment. Men who had the capital for deep-water fishing were rewarded with more and larger fish, thereby receiving more income than accrued to the individual fishermen, who, lacking boats, stood in the shallow water to cast their nets where the smaller fish were found. James' fishing crew included five men as well as hired servants.

Successful in business, respected in his community, congenial to his companions, James gave the impression of success and satisfaction. Yet there was in his heart, as in the hearts of his companions, a longing that the good things of life had not filled. His discontent showed itself in his interest in John the Baptist.

This preacher John, with his arresting personality and vivid proclamation of a Messiah whose coming would bring in the Kingdom of God, aroused the people as they had not been aroused for generations. His messianic message matched the mood of the day. Long had the people of Israel looked for the coming of One who would be their Saviour, but never had the desire been more intense than in the century immediately preceding John's advent. However, there was wide divergence in opinion as to the kind of Messiah expected. Some looked for a warrior king who, sent by God as savior for the nation, would conquer the national enemies and rule over his chosen people. Others, especially the priestly class, rejected the warrior savior, and forsook political ambition for religious hope. They looked for the Kingdom of God to come when all Israel perfectly obeyed the law even for a single day. Still others, who must have been numerous judging by the amount of literature they produced, looked for a supernatural intervention with God's savior coming on a cloud to impose his will on mankind through punishment of the unjust and blessing of the righteous.

Despite differences of opinion, widespread interest in a Divine Saviour provided a public mind especially receptive to a messianic message. The appearance of an authentic voice from God, as John the Baptist's was recognized to be, proclaiming that the Kingdom of God was at hand, stirred the masses, including James, to a fever of expectancy.

James listened eagerly as John the Baptist called for repentance and righteousness in preparation for the coming of the Messiah. When John offered baptism as a sign of renunciation of sin and dedication to the new life of the Kingdom, James, along with John, Peter, and Andrew, was among the first to accept the challenge and to be immersed in the cleansing waters.

After his baptism James and his partners seized every opportunity to listen to John the Baptist. The Gospel of John tells how two of the partners were directed by the Baptist to a stranger whom he called "the Lamb of God." Andrew, one of the two, went at once and brought Peter to Jesus. The other partner, not identified in the Gospel story, could have been John, who in turn brought James to share in the transfer of allegiance from John the Baptist to Jesus, "the Lamb of God." This conjecture is strengthened by the fact that their later call to discipleship, recorded in the first three Gospels, indicates that Peter, Andrew, James, and John were called as a group. Uncertain as these details are, it is well known that the four men shared the deeper aspirations of the spirit as well as a common occupation. As they toiled over the nets, they no doubt spent long hours talking about John the Baptist and Jesus, "the Lamb of God," wondering what it all meant for themselves and for the future of the people of Israel.

Some time after John the Baptist had pointed out Jesus to them, James and his brother John were in the boat with their father Zebedee, mending nets. A short distance away Simon and Andrew were casting their nets into the sea. Jesus walked by where they were working. Stopping first with Peter and Andrew, he said, "Follow me, and I will make you fishers of men." Immediately, the account has it, they left their nets and followed him. Walking on, Jesus came upon James and John, and called them. They, too, Matthew recounts, left the boat and their father and followed him.

Luke tells the story in a slightly different form. He says the fishermen were washing their nets when Jesus, pressed by a multitude of people, came to the place where they were working. Getting into Simon's boat, Jesus asked him to put out a little from the land, thus keeping the crowd at a distance so that he could the better speak to the four. As he ceased speaking he said to Simon, "Put out into the deep and let down your nets for a catch." Simon replied, "Master, we toiled all night and took nothing! But at your word I will let down the nets." When they were let down, the catch of fish was so great that the nets were at the breaking point and Simon had to call upon his partners to bring another boat to help. Both boats became so loaded with the enormous volume of fish that they began to sink. Peter, seeing the hand of God in this miraculous catch, fell at Jesus' feet and exclaimed, "Depart from me, for I am a sinful man." Jesus replied, "Do not be afraid, henceforth you will be catching men." When they had brought their boats to land, all four of the fishermen, James, Peter, Andrew, and John, left everything to follow the "Lamb of God."

The specific calls of three other disciples, Matthew, Philip, and Nathanael, are briefly recorded in the Gospels. Of the call of the other five apostles there is no record. The detail given to the call of the four fishermen is an early indication of their great importance in the Gospel story.

In addition to the disciples known by name there was a group of perhaps twenty or twenty-five others also called to discipleship. While we do not know exactly how many were invited to join the band, we do know that Jesus chose a group large enough to give a basis for selection of the Twelve.

For a period of weeks the band of disciples lived closely with Jesus. During this time, the Gospel of Matthew tells us, they saw Jesus heal a leper, the centurion's servant, Peter's wife's mother, the Gadarene demoniac, a paralytic, a woman with an issue of blood, a daughter believed dead, two blind men, and a dumb demoniac. In addition the disciples received verbal instruction, some of which Matthew gathered together in what is called the Sermon on the Mount.

After some months Jesus apparently realized the need of a smaller group to work closely with him. Which men to choose? He decided to take this crucial problem to his Father, so he "went out into the hills to pray; and all night he continued in prayer to God. And when it was day, he called his disciples, and chose from them twelve, whom he named apostles." James was one of this group.

After choosing the Twelve, Jesus began another important phase of their training. Master teacher that he was, he knew that the apostles needed more than demonstration and verbal instruction. The best way to learn, he realized, was by doing. So he sent the newly chosen apostles forth to heal the sick, raise the dead, cleanse the lepers, cast out demons, and teach and preach in the cities. They were to receive no sort of pay for their good deeds. Rather, their living was to be provided freely by those among whom they worked.

Jesus warned them that they were not to expect kind treatment, but flogging and persecution. The fact that these persecutions did not materialize until after his death gives rise to the suspicion that this advice is a later interpolation. However, it is possible that Jesus admonished the apostles knowing that persecution was inevitable and hoping to prepare them for it.

Some students of the Bible hold that in all Jesus taught and did he had in mind the specific training of the Twelve. When we turn from the Gospels to the history of the early Church, this assumption does not seem to be too wide of the mark, for certainly the apostles were tried instruments which God could use to carry the Gospel after Jesus' death. By the end of the first century, largely through their efforts, He was known and loved over much of the known world.

Some facts about the family from which James came are

known; other information is inferred. James was probably an older brother of John, an inference drawn from the fact that his name precedes John's in all the lists of the apostles. The name of their father, Zebedee, appears only at the time of their call. It has been suggested that it was because Zebedee raised such a storm of protest over losing two successful fishermen from the family business that Jesus called James and John "Sons of Thunder," although it may be only that Zebedee had a tumultuous nature. Failure to mention Zebedee further may reasonably be attributed to the lack of adequate records of people not germane to the Gospel story. It is more probable, as will be shown, that the term Sons of Thunder was used by Jesus to describe the sons themselves rather than the father.

The mother of James and John, Salome, was a follower of Jesus and present at his Crucifixion. This relationship of Salome to the two apostles is revealed by a comparison of the lists of the women about the Cross as given in Mark and in Matthew. Also it is commonly assumed that Salome was the sister of Mary, the mother of Jesus. This assumption is based on comparison of the lists in Mark and Matthew with the one in John, who mentions four women present at the Crucifixion: the mother of Jesus; her sister; Mary, wife of Clopas; and Mary Magdalene. It is most probable that the sister of Jesus' mother is the Salome of the earlier lists, and that Mary, the wife of Clopas, is the same person as the mother of James and Joses. Although these identifications are not beyond question, they are perhaps the best that can be made from the uncertain data available.* James and John thus become cousins of Jesus. If this relationship existed they must have had frequent contact with Jesus far earlier than any record we have in Scripture, and their knowledge of each other was surely extensive even before the public ministry of our Lord.

The fact that all lists of the apostles give Peter, Andrew, James, and John the first four places suggests that James was one

* See Chapter 10 for further discussion of the identity of Mary, wife of Clopas.

of the leaders of the Twelve. In three instances when Jesus took a small group apart, James was included along with Peter and John: at the healing of Jairus' daughter, at the Transfiguration of Jesus, and at the time of the prayer in the inner Garden of Gethsemane.

The affection which Jesus had for these disciples did not keep him from realizing their shortcomings. That "Sons of Thunder" was an appropriate appellation for James and John is illustrated by two incidents. On one occasion, when a Samaritan village refused to receive Jesus, James burst out, "Lord, do you want us to bid fire come down from heaven and consume them as Elijah did?" His reference was to the story, familiar to all Jews, of the prophet who destroyed two bands of fifty soldiers each which had been sent to capture him because he had rebuked King Ahaziah. But Jesus rebuked James, telling him he did not understand the new teaching; the purpose of the Son of Man was not to destroy men's lives but to save them.

James' explosive nature not yet quelled, he later joined his brother in a brash request. "Grant us to sit, one at your right hand and one at your left, in your glory." Jesus used this occasion to speak about the meaning of suffering as it relates to glory; then he went on to speak to them of service. "Whoever would be first among you must be slave of all," he said. The glory in the Kingdom of God, he added, is the glory of suffering for a cause and of serving the common good. Over and over he repeated this lesson to the disciples, but only after the Crucifixion did its truth begin to dawn upon them.

That only these two sentences spoken by James are recorded leads some Bible students to conclude that he was a silent man. But the inference that a man was silent simply because his words are not in a written record is quite illogical. Besides, Jesus called James "Son of Thunder" and it is difficult to think of silent thunder.

Taking a different point of view, Jerome interpreted the phrase as referring to James' supreme ability as a preacher. But the fact that James preached very little until after the death of

Jesus makes it unlikely that Jesus would have characterized him by an unused skill. Zeal for the Lord, ambition for the Kingdom, bigness of voice, and bigness of mind and action—these are the more likely characteristics that won for James the title "Son of Thunder."

James is not mentioned in the Gospel of John, a fact of especial interest if we accept John, the brother of James, as its author. The Gospel of John is the only source of information about Philip, Andrew, and Nathanael Bartholomew. Yet strangely enough, John tells nothing of James, his brother, and conceals his own identity under the cloak of "the beloved disciple." The usual explanation of these omissions is the reticence of John; but, even so, they seem unnatural and difficult to understand. This is one of many portions of the Bible record about which more knowledge is needed.

On the day of Pentecost James was present to receive the outpouring of the Holy Spirit, and in the stirring days that followed he was a leader of the developing church. The Book of Acts gives details of the preaching of Peter and John which aroused the growing opposition of the religious leaders of the Jews. As the opposition grew these two were imprisoned, Stephen was stoned, and Saul began a systematic persecution of the Christians. Unable to control the growth of the Christian faith by the means at their disposal, the religious leaders of the Jews sought the help of Rome, finally persuading Herod to take a hand in destroying this new heresy. In 42 A.D. James' name appears in a tragic story. "Herod the king laid violent hands upon some who belonged to the church. He killed James the brother of John with the sword." Why should Herod have selected James to become the first victim of his persecution? Although the record is silent, it seems reasonable to assume that James had been exercising noticeable leadership that made the enemies of the Church desire his death. When a man wants to eradicate a despised sect he does not begin with the last man in the rear column. He takes someone near the top. Herod struck the man who counted, knowing that his blow would silence even a Son of Thunder. The blow did indeed put an early end to a forceful Christian leader, and made James the first apostolic martyr.

His life cut short, James had little time to impress the force of his personality upon the early Church, but he has come alive in tradition with such vigor that his influence on the events of the early Middle Ages, especially in Spain, gives him a place of peculiar distinction. A peninsula of the European continent, Spain was shut off from her neighbor to the north by a natural barrier, the Pyrenees Mountains. On the south she was separated from Africa by a strip of water only nine miles wide. This strategic location made her the early meeting place for the cultures of Europe and Africa.

The process by which the country was Christianized is not clear. Paul in his letter to the Romans spoke of his desire to carry the Gospel to Spain. Most scholars believe that his martyrdom prevented him from fulfilling this desire, but there are some who think that he did go to Spain. The Spanish tradition, however, is that the apostle James founded the Christian Church there. Although his early death makes this conclusion almost untenable, the legend has exercised great influence on the Spanish people. Historians generally assign the beginning of Christianity in Spain to the second or third century. But no one can be sure about this early period, for there are no trustworthy sources of information.

Spain, like most of Europe, was under Roman domination from the first century before Christ until the breakdown of the Empire in the fifth century of the Christian era. When the barbarian hordes swept over the Roman dominions, Spain, like the rest of the Empire, was overrun. Her life did not differ greatly from that in other parts of Europe until the seventh century, when the followers of Mohammed, sword in one hand and the Koran in the other, swept over Syria, Palestine, Mesopotamia, Persia, Egypt, and North Africa. In the East only Constantinople was able to withstand the power of their onslaught. In the year 711 Spain was invaded by Tarik, who gave the name Gibraltar (from *jabal* [Arabic for mount] and Tarik) to the rock upon which his troops landed for their victorious march over the peninsula. Not content with the conquest of Spain, the Moslems pressed on into France, until Charles Martel and Pepin the Short ended their expansion by decisive military action first at Tours in 732 and later by a series of battles that drove them back across the Pyrenees to Spain. There Moslem rule fixed itself so firmly that the last control was not broken until the victories of Ferdinand and Isabella in 1492.

With the Moslem armies came their religion. People were not compelled to accept Mohammedanism but many inducements were offered to win converts. Christians paid poll taxes but Moslems did not; Christian slaves on being converted to Mohammedanism were set free. To these direct benefits was added the appeal of the genuine superiority of the Moslem in the arts, irrigation, agriculture, medicine, and various processes of manufacturing. Public buildings testified to the excellence of Moslem architecture and ornamentation. Cordova, the largest and most prosperous city in Spain, built a mosque with nineteen gateways of bronze, 4,700 lamps fed by perfumed oil, and 1,200 columns of porphyry, jasper, and marble. Its sanctuary was paved with silver and its pulpit made of 36,000 separate panels of ivory and rare wood encrusted with precious stones and fastened with gold nails. Besides being one of the most magnificent buildings in the world at that time, this mosque had on its central altar the left heel of the prophet Mohammed. Such a holy relic, along with the startling beauty of the place of worship, brought more than one Christian first to admire, then to debate, and finally to embrace the Mohammedan faith. In the ninth century the future for the Christian Church in Spain looked very dark indeed. How this challenge was met and the part that the apostle James played in the drama, centuries after his death, is one of the most exciting stories in the pseudohistory of Christianity.

In Iria Flavia, modern El Padron, a small wind-swept, rock-bound seaport on the northeast coast of Spain, a group of Christian hermits lived their quiet, uneventful life of poverty and prayer. The most devoted and venerable of them was Palagio. One night as Palagio and his hermit brothers gathered for prayer, they saw an exceedingly bright star lighting up the scene. On succeeding nights the star continued to appear and many little stars seemed to wander and flicker through the landscape. As the hermits watched in amazement they heard voices softly singing marvelous antiphons and anthems, such as are sung in praise before the High Altar of God.

The more the simple men pondered these phenomena, the more puzzled they became. In search for guidance they told their story to Bishop Theodomirus, who at once saw the hand of God at work and ordered three days of fasting and prayer. Then the Bishop, the hermits, and some shepherds and citizens of Iria Flavia set out to find the cause of these visitations. At last they ascertained the spot from which the light and music seemed to come, a wild bit of land overspread with dense thickets. By strenuous effort the ground was cleared and the entrance to a cave was uncovered. As they entered the cave, they came upon a small altar beneath an arch supported by pillars. Here was a sarcophagus covered with a stone slab. When the slab was removed a sweet, fragrant odor emerged—certain sign that here was the body of a saint. Beside the tomb was a letter written in good Spanish: "Here lies Santiago, son of Zebedee and Salome, brother of St. John, whom Herod beheaded in Jerusalem." The date of the discovery of the tomb was July 25, 813, since commemorated as the feast day of St. James.

Word was taken at once to King Alfonso II and Emperor Charlemagne, who gathered together the nobles of Spain. Tremendous consequences were at stake not only for Spain but for the entire world.

The body was placed first in the Benedictine monastery of San Pedro de Antealtares, about four leagues inland from Iria Flavia. When this humble place could no longer serve such a high purpose, King Alfonso II before his death in 842, ordered the body of James to be moved to Compostela. For its shrine he gave three miles of land in every direction; twenty years later the grant was increased to six miles. Christians all over Spain contributed to the shrine, so that it early achieved great wealth and influence. Mohammedan Cordova suffered a setback, for what was the left heel of Mohammed compared to the whole body of an apostle of Jesus Christ? Let Asia Minor claim John, and Rome have Peter; by the goodness of God, the Christians in Moorish-occupied Spain were blessed with the body of James.

The resting place of St. James came to be called Santiago (Saint Iago or Saint James) de Compostela, field of the stars. As such it became a shrine that rivaled Rome and Jerusalem in attracting pilgrims. In Western Europe it was especially popular, for it had the advantage of being closer, less expensive, and less dangerous to reach than the more distant shrines. Boatloads of pilgrims came from England and France. Thousands came by horseback or on foot. The psychological victory for Christianity assumed enormous proportions as pilgrims crowded to Santiago de Compostela to receive forgiveness of sins and healing for their sicknesses. Throughout the Middle Ages, as its fame grew, chains of hostels were established to look after the pilgrims, and orders developed whose special duty it was to care for the religious folk who made the sacred pilgrimage. Commerce and trade were greatly stimulated. By the thirteenth century pilgrimages to Compostela ranked on a level with those to Rome or to Jerusalem, and in 1478 Pope Sixtus IV officially gave to pilgrimages to Compostela the same status as those to Rome or to Jerusalem.

When the Crusades began in 1096, Spain was under the control of the Mohammedans, and knights who volunteered to help Spain fight her Moslem conquerors were excused from the Jerusalem Crusades. In the battles of Calavijo, 846; Simancus, 939; and Alcoras, 1096, St. James himself is said to have appeared to lead the Spanish warriors to success. Stimulated by his inspiration, the country liberated more and more of its territory from Moslem control.

The task of liberation was complete in 1492. Americans think of this as the year in which our continent was discovered, but in that year Ferdinand and Isabella, without any idea of the value of the discovery by Columbus, celebrated the final victory over the Moors by ordering a thank offering to Compostela of a bushel of grain for every pair of oxen, horses, mules, and asses used in agriculture throughout Spain.

To account for the miraculous presence of the bones of James in Spain, legends grew up relating his adventures prior to the discovery of his body. The story has it that after the day of Pentecost he went to Spain to carry the Gospel. At Saragossa, weary with his effort to win converts, he fell asleep, and as he slept the Virgin Mary appeared to him and told him to build a chapel in her honor on that very spot. Another night while conversing with some disciples James saw lights and heard singing. Looking to heaven, he saw the Virgin Mary on a throne sustained by a host of angels. By her side was a column of jasper and a wooden image of herself. She ordered a chapel erected in her honor. "For," she said, "this place is to be my house, my right inheritance and possession. This image and column of mine shall be the title and altar of the temple you shall build."

So St. James built the church and the Blessed Virgin often came to worship there. *La gloriosa colonna,* the Spanish call their heavenly gift. Thousands and tens of thousands have visited Saragossa's Church of St. Mary of the Pillar with its jasper pillar and the black figure of the Virgin. Worshipers still crowd this shrine, one of the most venerated in all Spain. As early as 1200 Pope Innocent III declared, "God alone can count the miracles which are here performed."

Naturally, Saragossa was made a bishopric. Its first Bishop was said to have been Athanasius, a Greek born in Toledo, converted at Jerusalem, and a companion of St. James on his voyage to Spain. The legendary name of Saragossa is "Happy Other World." As befits such a lovely name, it is said that in this city neither fruits nor corn ever spoil and no reptile or serpent can live.

Another story tells that St. James founded the church at Mugia, a desolate spot near Cape Finisterre, which then indeed seemed the end of the world. The walls of the church at Caldas de Reyes depict in relief the story of James' arrival at Mugia in a boat guided by a figure, half girl and half swan. The Virgin Mary accompanied him, and when she stepped out of the boat her footprint was fixed in granite rock. This stone is still preserved in the Church of Nuestra Señora de la Barca, a favorite pilgrim shrine at Mugia.

An even greater wonder: by the sea below the church is preserved the ship in which St. James arrived. The ship, turned to stone, is raised a few inches from the rocky surface of the shore and at certain times appears to sway slightly with the waves. The sail is likewise preserved in stone, and people crawl upon it to kiss the stone and perform other rites held to be a cure for certain diseases.

However St. James got to Spain and wherever he landed, tradition agrees that he traveled over the peninsula from city to city and from town to town, establishing numerous bishoprics, starting many orders, building churches, and converting multitudes of people.

Improbable as is any chronological story based upon the various legends, another must be added to complete the record of James' experiences. After his missionary work in Spain legend returns him to Jerusalem, where he was killed by Herod. The disciples then took the body from Jerusalem, for fear of the Jews, and placed it on a ship without sail or rudder. In seven days the angels of the Lord miraculously conveyed the ship to Iria Flavia in Spain. When the voyagers reached their destination they saw a man riding on the seashore; his restless horse plunged into the sea and then walked on the crest of the waves toward them. As they watched in amazement, both horse and rider suddenly sank beneath the water, appearing after a brief time covered over with lovely white-lined scallop shells. The scallop shell thus became the emblem of St. James. For centuries craftsmen have mounted the shells as talismans to guard from harm those who seek the apostle's shrine. The man on the horse, said to be a bridegroom, went joyfully on to his wedding.

The ship bearing the body of James reached land, whereupon

the body was lifted out and placed on a stone beside the sea. The stone, as if it had been soft wax, hollowed itself out to make a coffin for the holy man. Soon afterward a faithful disciple, or perhaps some pagan fishermen who had respect for the dead, removed the body to higher ground and there it rested for eight hundred years. Here the body was discovered by the devout hermits and James became a dominant influence on Spanish religious history for succeeding centuries.

Since James was supposed to have done so much to inspire the Spanish people in their struggle for freedom and to bring Spain favorably before the Christian world, he was naturally made her patron saint. National affection for him is more than shallow sentimentality; it combines such love as the people of the United States have for George Washington with the deep religious devotion accorded a saint.

In our day it is difficult to realize that James' influence over Spain is verifiable history, legendary though the stories are. Modern man cannot understand how the discovery of a long-dead person's bones could arouse so much passion and action. But perhaps in our scientific age the temptation is to believe too little rather than too much. In contrast, during the Middle Ages few people could read or write, much less understand history or set up scientific standards of fact. It was an age of faith, of stress on the miraculous, and of reliance on authority. The people of Spain and of Europe were as ready to believe that the body of James was discovered in Iria Flavia on July 25, 813, as the people of the modern world were to accept the announcement of the atomic bomb that fell on Hiroshima on August 6, 1945. Both discoveries fitted the mood of their day and both released vast new energies.

Eusebius, quoting from Clement of Alexandria, who lived about 175 A.D., retells another ancient tradition about James. According to him a man later tradition named Josias brought the accusation against James that caused him to be condemned to death by Herod; but when Josias saw the apostle's conduct at his trial he was deeply moved, fell down before him, and asked acceptance into the Christian faith and forgiveness for his false accusation. James gave him the kiss of forgiveness with the words *pax vobiscum,* "Peace be with you." After the death of James, Josias quickly paid the price of his new faith with his own life.

Thus the man called by Jesus "Son of Thunder" ended his life with a kiss of forgiveness and a word of blessing on his lips. James, the first apostolic martyr, died in the spirit of his Lord and Master.

5 John, Beloved Son of Thunder

SAINT JOHN'S DAY December 27

The Collect

Merciful Lord, we beseech thee to cast thy bright beams of light upon thy Church, that it, being illumined by the doctrine of thy blessed Apostle and Evangelist Saint John, may so walk in the light of thy truth, that it may at length attain to life everlasting; through Jesus Christ our Lord. *Amen.*

THE CROWD PRESSED IN, THOSE ON THE EDGES STANDing on tiptoe and stretching their necks to see what was going on at the center. John, son of Zebedee, attracted by the crowd, drew near also and heard a loud voice crying out, "In the name of Jesus of Nazareth come out of him." Pushing his way through the crowd, he saw a man casting out demons. Upon inquiry he discovered that although the man used the name of Jesus to cast out the demons, he was not one of the followers of Jesus. Whereupon John sternly ordered the man to cease his healing. Expecting approval for his zeal, he hastened to tell Jesus what he had done. To his surprise, Jesus rebuked him, "Do not forbid him; for he that is not against us is for us." Unlike John, Jesus was evidently not interested in excluding anyone from good works for lack of proper credentials.

A few days later, at the end of a weary journey, Jesus sent messengers into a Samaritan village to seek hospitality. When the messengers returned they reported every door closed to travelers headed for Jerusalem. This rebuff gave rise to the angry question raised by James, the other Son of Thunder, "Shall we call down fire from heaven?" For lack of comment from John we judge that he evidently shared his brother's misunderstanding of Jesus' motives.

These events, near the end of Jesus' ministry, call to mind the childish request which John and James had made earlier in the Gospel story. "Teacher," they asked, "will you grant us whatever we ask of you?"

Jesus, too wise to grant such a sweeping request, asked, "What exactly do you want?"

"Grant us," they said, "to sit one on your right hand and one on your left in your glory."

"You do not know what you are asking," Jesus replied. "Are you able to drink the cup that I am to drink?"

With a glibness that betrayed their lack of understanding, they answered, "We are able."

Looking to the future and the shadow of the Cross, Jesus said, "The cup I drink you will drink but to sit at my right hand and at my left is not mine to grant, but it is for those for whom it has been prepared by my Father."

Presumptuous questions these brothers asked; but such presumption is not uncommon, for there is more of the Son of Thunder in human nature than most people like to admit. The undisciplined ego is continually self-seeking.

Undisciplined as was this Son of Thunder, he none the less possessed vigorous emotional drive, deep feeling, and a passionate impulse to action—attributes which Jesus needed in his followers. What He wanted done could not be accomplished by tea-and-crumpets leaders. Strong men can make terrible blunders, as did John; but they may be capable of complete commitment. His later development makes it clear that John became the disciple whom Jesus loved, a mystic and the Apostle of Love. "The beloved disciple" remained as vigorous and as deeply passionate as in the days when he was first called the Son of Thunder. His emotional endowment was not changed, but he was inwardly disciplined and redirected by years of fellowship with his Lord.

At the time John was called to discipleship he was probably in his late teens. The late Bishop Francis J. McConnell has characterized that period of life as the green-apple stage. He used to say that he had heard poems about apple blossoms and about the ripe fruit on the tree, but that he had never heard a poem about green apples. However, Jesus knew that the green apple would ripen and that youthful John, committed to a cause in his youth, had possibilities for great achievement.

Because Jesus saw the spiritual capacity inherent in John, he gave him especial attention. He took him, along with Peter and James, when he raised the daughter of Jairus from death. On the Mount of Transfiguration John, again with Peter and James, saw the appearance of Jesus' countenance altered as he talked with Moses and Elijah. The three heard a heavenly voice proclaim, "This is my Son, my Chosen; listen to him." Through these experiences of crisis, as John came to a better understanding of the mind of the Master, he grew more like him. It was John and Peter whom Jesus chose to make ready the Passover for the Last Supper. Thus was his confidence shown.

The Gospel of John does not mention him by name. Rather, he is designated by the phrase "the disciple whom Jesus loved." Though there is no reference to John until the last night of Jesus' earthly life, all of the references show him as an ideal disciple. New Testament scholars have been disturbed at the transformation of the very human Son of Thunder into the ideal disciple, but it needs to be remembered that Son of Thunder was an early epithet and "beloved disciple" a characterization given near the end of the first century. Time softens the sharp edges of character and engraves for history the nobler aspects of personality. When the Gospel of John was written, John was the only living apostle, a venerable apostle of love. Which portrait has verisimilitude is not as important as the understanding that John's Gospel selected for the record only the incidents that revealed the character of the apostle as it had become at the time the Gospel was written.

"The beloved disciple" is mentioned five times in the Fourth Gospel. The first reference occurs at the Last Supper when Jesus told his disciples, "One of you will betray me." Peter asked John to inquire of the Lord, "Who is it?" because John, seated next to Jesus, was in a more favorable position to ask the question.

At the trial of Jesus there are reasons to believe that the term "another disciple," who was known to the High Priest and who had secured entrance for Peter to the trial, referred to John. If this is true, he was a second apostle present at Jesus' trial.

At Calvary John stood by the Cross. Indeed, he was the only apostle present at the Crucifixion. In his suffering Jesus turned to his mother and, indicating him, said, "Woman, behold your son"; then to "the beloved disciple," "Behold your mother." John, in obedience to Jesus' desire that his mother be spared his final hours of suffering, immediately took Mary to his home. Tradition says he cared for her until her death.

When, early in the morning on the first Easter Day, Mary Magdalene discovered that the tomb of Jesus did not contain his body, she hastened to report the fact to Peter and John, who ran to see for themselves that the tomb was empty. Some time later several of the apostles were fishing on Lake Galilee when in the early dawn a dim figure on the shore called to them. At first they thought the stranger was a villager seeking to buy fish, but when at his direction they cast the net on the right side of the ship and caught 153 fish, the "disciple whom Jesus loved" was the first to exclaim in joy, "It is the Lord." This early recognition is fully consistent with the other incidents recorded about John. More than any of the others "the beloved disciple" appears to have been spiritually sensitive and alive to revelation of higher truth.

On one occasion before his Crucifixion, after Jesus and the disciples had broken bread together beside the lake, Jesus three times questioned Peter about his love. Peter trying to divert attention from himself, asked, "Lord, what about this man?" referring to John. Jesus replied, "If it is my will that he remain until I come, what is that to you?" This answer gave rise to the mistaken idea that "the beloved disciple" would not die, but live until the Lord's return. Actually John did live to be a very old man and died near the end of the first century. If it is assumed that he was around twenty when Jesus died, he would have been between eighty and ninety at the time of his own death. Some tradition makes him even older. Since his long life was lived during the time when Christians were expecting the immediate return of Christ to judge the world, it is small wonder that the idea circulated that he would live until the Lord's return. Bishop John Phillip Newman makes the interesting comment that John "outlived twelve Roman Emperors, inclusive of Augustus and Nero, two of whom committed suicide, seven of whom were murdered, and nearly all of whom were persecutors of the religion which is now the hope and joy of humanity."

One better understands "the beloved disciple" by reading the Gospel of John and the three Epistles of John. Probably no book in the Bible is more loved and more read than the Gospel that bears his name. In Evanston, Illinois, the Bible of Frances Willard lies on a small table beside a comfortable chair in her home, which admirers have preserved as a shrine. This well-worn Bible reveals that the Gospel of John and the Psalms were her favorite books. This is probably true of most Bible readers.

Paul was the theologian who more than any other set the framework of thought for the Christian movement. But John was the mystic who spoke directly to the heart. Clement of Alexandria comments, "John, last, having observed that the bodily things had been set forth in the Gospels, and exhorted thereto by the Spirit, produced a spiritual Gospel." When Christians think of John, they think of spiritual matters: born anew, water of life, bread of life, light of the world, good shepherd, my Father's house, true vine. How deeply these symbols have fixed themselves in the minds and hearts of Christians everywhere!

Augustine comments that "John . . . soars like an eagle above the clouds of human infirmity, and gazes upon the light of unchangeable truth with those keen and steadiest eyes of the heart." People often come to the Christian religion for an answer to life's problems, but even more frequently they seek an elevation of spirit and a contact with eternal reality that will give depth and meaning to human experience. John gives such insight, such uplift. That explains why his Gospel is characterized by Augustine as the eagle, for the eagle alone is able to soar high above the clouds and look directly into the face of the sun.

The Gospel of John is one of the simplest and at the same time one of the most profound books in the Bible. It speaks to all ages, all groups, all centuries, all educational levels, and all human needs. Those who go to it in need come away with their cup overflowing. Return as often as they will, the supply never diminishes.

Have any words ever inspired a sense of God's presence more than these from the Gospel of John?

> God is Spirit, and those who worship him must worship in spirit and truth.
>
> It is the spirit that gives life, the flesh is of no avail; the words that I have spoken to you are spirit and life.
>
> I am the resurrection and the life; he who believes in me, though he die, yet shall he live, and whoever lives and believes in me shall never die.
>
> Let not your hearts be troubled; believe in God, believe also in me. In my Father's house are many rooms; if it were not so, would I have told you that I go to prepare a place for you? And when I go and prepare a place for you, I will come again and will take you to myself, that where I am you may be also.
>
> I am the bread of life; he who comes to me shall not hunger, and he who believes in me shall never thirst.

Among the most loved words in all the Bible are:

God so loved the world that he gave his only Son, that whoever believes in him should not perish but have eternal life.

The Epistles of John are written by the same author as the Gospel of John. The impression of the author formed in the Gospel is strengthened in the Epistles, which contain a profound statement of the gospel of love as the Christian way of life.

Little children, let us not love in word or speech but in deed and in truth.

We know that we have passed out of death into life, because we love the brethren.

The great passage in the fourth chapter of First John begins with the injunction:

Beloved, let us love one another; for love is of God, and he who loves is born of God and knows God.

and ends with the declaration that:

He who loves God should love his brother also.

Aside from Paul's hymn of love in First Corinthians, no passage in the Scripture equals these words as a description of Christian love. In the First Epistle of John the word "love" is used more than fifty times and "beloved" is the beautiful word used to describe fellow Christians.

The authorship of the books in the Bible that bear John's name presents one of the most difficult problems in the study of the New Testament. Prior to 1800 no one questioned but that the apostle John wrote the Gospel of John, the three Epistles of John, and the Revelation. Since 1800 the question of authorship of these books has been the subject of exhaustive research; in fact, an estimated one thousand scholarly works have been written on the subject. However, there is still no established basis of fact for judgment. The most radical scholarship denies that John can be identified with the author of any New Testament books. The most conservative scholars believe that he is the author of all five books. An intermediate position recognizes John as one important source of the material found in the Gospel of John and the Epistles but sees in these writings, in their present form, the editorial supervision of an unknown author. If this reasonable position is accepted, the material in the Gospel of John and the Epistles of John can rightly be used to throw light on the character of the apostle. The book of Revelation, most modern scholars hold, was not written by the same author as the Gospel and the Epistles of John.

Since the recent discovery of the Dead Sea Scrolls there has been conjecture on the part of some scholars that the author of the Gospel of John may have been a member of the Essene sect and that the Gospel might have been written in the latter part of the first century. This theory is based upon the parallelism of certain words and ideas in the Gospel of John with those in the Essene Manual of Discipline. For example, John says, "He was in the beginning with God; all things were made through him, and without him was not anything made that was made": while the Manual of Discipline reads, "And by his knowledge everything has been brought into being. And everything that is, he established by his purpose; and apart from him, nothing is done." Conclusions in this field need more mature study before they can be accepted with confidence.

No one can glance at the literature on the authorship of books accredited to John without being impressed with the diligence, the sincerity, the piety, and the learning of the scholars who have wrestled with the issue. The nature of the problem rather than lack of serious effort leaves the question open for further research.

Following the Resurrection, John shared with the other apostles the fifty days of waiting for the coming of the Holy Spirit. In the upper room on the day of Pentecost he was one of those upon whom tongues of fire appeared, and being filled with the Holy Spirit he began to speak in tongues. He shared in rejoicing at the remarkable results of this outpouring of the Spirit which won for the Church three thousand souls in a single day.

After Pentecost John and Peter healed a lame man at the Beautiful Gate of the Temple. As a reward for this deed and the sermon that followed they were arrested and thrown into prison for a night. Brought before the rulers and elders they gave a vigorous defense of the Gospel of Jesus Christ. Shocked at the boldness of John and Peter and thinking them common, uneducated men, polluted by contact with Jesus, the rulers threatened them with severe punishment if they did not cease preaching, then released them. Undaunted, John and Peter replied, "Whether it is right in the sight of God to listen to you rather than to God, you must judge; for we cannot but speak of what we have seen and heard." They continued to preach.

After a brief period of public preaching John and Peter were again arrested and put in the common prison, but an angel delivered them during the night and the very next day they preached Christ in the Temple. Wearied with half measures and discouraged with their efforts to silence the voices of the apostles by intimidation, some members of the Synagogue of the Freedmen next brought Stephen before the Council and accused him of heresy. Stephen was found guilty and stoned to death. This was the beginning of a great persecution against the Church in Jerusalem. John stayed there with the apostles and faced their common danger.

Here he became a consultant on many problems pertaining to Church policy. When Philip, the Evangelist, was in Samaria he proclaimed Christ to the Samaritans with such power that many believed and were baptized. Signs and great miracles accompanied the proclamation of the Gospel. Later, when word of Philip's success reached Jerusalem, John and Peter were appointed to investigate the new wonder. Upon arrival they found the reports to be accurate. As they prayed and laid their hands on the new converts the Holy Spirit descended upon them, establishing beyond doubt that God was at work among the Samaritans. How significant that John, who had once wished to call down fire to destroy an inhospitable Samaritan village, was chosen to pray and to lay his hands on the Samaritans that they might receive the life-giving Holy Spirit!

The conversion of the Samaritans and other Gentiles soon gave rise to the question of the relation of these new converts to the Jewish laws, especially the law of circumcision. Apostles and elders of the Church gathered at Jerusalem to consider this problem in the first great Christian conference. It is logical to assume that John was one of the apostles attending this conference in Jerusalem. His attitude toward the Samaritan converts and the record of his previous approval of Paul's missionary activity seem to indicate that he joined in approving the decision to liberate Gentile converts from the necessity of observing the Mosaic law of ceremonial purification.

The Scripture record of John ends with the first Church Council. Beyond that Augustine states that John preached to the Parthians. Tertullian says that John was with Peter in Rome and that after a miraculous delivery from a caldron of boiling oil he went to Ephesus. There is also a tradition that an attempt was made to poison John, but that when he took the cup the poison disappeared in the form of a serpent. Thus the symbol for this apostle is a cup with a serpent issuing from it. Polycrates and Irenaeus state that John was a priest and wore the high priestly miter, but the variance of this late tradition with the known fact that John was a fisherman makes it of doubtful value. The second book of Papias states that John was probably killed near the time of the death of his brother James (42 A.D.). Scholars who deny John's authorship of the books that bear his name express great interest in this tradition. If John died about 42 he could not possibly have written these books, for most scholars agree that they were written near the end of the first century. Overwhelming tradition, almost universally accepted, gives John a long life and makes him Bishop of Ephesus during his last days.

Unfortunately the years between 70 and 110 A.D. are among the most obscure portions of church history, shrouding much desirable information about John. It is known that the Christian movement grew rapidly during this time. Although the Church gained its membership largely from the lower classes, by 100 A.D. it was a significant force in Asia Minor, Syria, Macedonia, Greece, Rome, and probably also in Egypt. It had expanded slightly toward the Western portions of the Empire and, if tradition is to be trusted, to Eastern lands as distant as India. The influx of non-Christians into the early Church posed a great problem for the preservation of the purity of the Gospel as is revealed in the New Testament and in other extant literature on the period. The destruction of Jerusalem in 70 A.D. effectively destroyed its influence and bequeathed to Ephesus, Rome, and Antioch the responsibility for leading the fast-growing Christian Church. Ephesus, the largest and most influential city of larger Asia Minor, was more extensively Christianized than any other area. Naturally, this gave Ephesus a commanding position in the early Church. The work of Paul, Apollos, Timothy, John Mark, Aquila, and Priscilla laid a firm foundation that John used to advantage. Under him, Ephesus was second to no other city in its influence for the Gospel.

Three stories told about John during his stay in Ephesus gather together the knowledge we have of him during that period. It is known that Ephesus was a center of the Gnostic heresy and that one of the purposes of the First Epistle of John was to combat this heresy. One day John went into a public bathhouse and to his surprise found Cerinthus, leader of the heretical movement, there. John rushed out of the bathhouse without bathing, crying out, "Let us fly, lest even the bathhouse fall on us." "Do you know who I am?" asked Cerinthus. "I know you are the first-born of the Devil," said John, giving evidence that he had not entirely outgrown attributes of the youthful Son of Thunder.

Clement of Alexandria tells that in a city near Ephesus John found a young man "strong of body, beautiful in appearance, and warm of heart" and won him for Christ. When John left the city he publicly commended the youth to the Bishop for pastoral care. Later John returned and inquired about the youthful convert. In great embarrassment the Bishop had to report, "He is dead." "How and by what death?" John inquired. "He has died to God," was the reply, "for he turned out wicked and abandoned and, in short, a robber. Now, instead of to the church, he has taken to the mountains with a band of men like himself." The apostle rent his clothes and with great lamentation beat his head. "A fine guard," he said, "did I leave for the soul of our brother. But, now, let a horse be furnished for me, and let someone show me the way." He started at once to look for the young man. Guards posted by the bandit brought John to the young man, who, when he saw the aged apostle, fled in shame. "Why, my child, do you flee from me, your own father, unarmed and old?" called out John. "Pity me, child, have no fear. You still have hope of life. I shall give an account for you to Christ. If need be, I will willingly endure your death, just as the Lord did for us. I shall give up my life for you. Stop, believe, Christ has sent me." The robber stood and, weeping bitterly, fell into the arms of the aged apostle, who restored him with tenderness to the fellowship of the Church. Small wonder that such a man was called the Apostle of Love.

Jerome recounts that the aged John, highly respected as the only apostle still alive and the author of four popular books, was invited on one First Day to preach in the church at Ephesus. His coming was widely publicized and on the appointed day a vast multitude assembled, filling every available place in the church and the area around it.

When John arrived he was so feeble that he had to be carried into the church. After eloquent words of welcome and a lengthy preparatory service, such as prominent people are ever subjected to, John was lifted to his feet to speak. A great hush came over the congregation. Everyone strained to hear each word. The aged man said, "Little children, love one another, love one another, love one another." He sat down, his sermon over. Many went home disappointed. They shook their heads and said, "It is too bad the old man is in his dotage. Why doesn't he stop trying to preach?"

But others realized that simple as the aged apostle's sermon may have seemed, it contained the heart of the Gospel. It is the insight of the saint, not the infirmity of the senile, that says, "Little children, love one another!"

6
Philip of Bethsaida

ST. PHILIP'S DAY May 1

The Collect

O Almighty God, whom truly to know is everlasting life; Grant us perfectly to know thy Son Jesus Christ to be the way, the truth, and the life; that, following the steps of thy holy Apostles, Saint Philip and Saint James, we may stedfastly walk in the way that leadeth to eternal life; through the same thy Son Jesus Christ our Lord. *Amen.*

IMAGINE A SCENE WHERE A PROUD JEWISH FATHER receives a boy child in his arms and pronounces his name, "Philip." The orthodox lift an eyebrow and whisper, "Why not Jacob, Isaac, David, or some other good Jewish name? There is too much acceptance of Greek ways and Greek names. If this goes on, what is to become of our religion and our race?" But the father has an especial reason for choosing the name and, whispers or no whispers, it remains.

Philip was the name of the tetrarch of Ituraea. The birthplace of the child, Bethsaida, a city on Lake Galilee at the mouth of the River Jordan, was the capital of Ituraea. The boy's father remembered that a decade ago this village of Bethsaida was exactly what its name signified—"Fishhouse"; but after ten years under the rule of Philip the tetrarch, Bethsaida was not "Fishhouse" but Bethsaida Julias, the proud capital of a province, and bearer of the name of the daughter of the Emperor Augustus. The ten years of Philip's rule had brought soldiers, public officials, traders, and builders to the village. Many buildings had been erected; a palace for the governor, offices for the government business, barracks for soldiers, and residences to house the swelling population. Prosperity had come to Bethsaida with Philip the tetrarch.

From his father Philip received more than a Greek name. He was given a home receptive to new ideas and appreciative of new cultural influences. Doubtless he learned the language from which his name was derived. He learned something of the ways of people who came from far-off lands and had traditions which differed from those of his Jewish parents. He was delivered from rigid orthodoxy that closes the mind to new truth.

But Philip's Greek name did not hinder his loyalty to the Jewish religion. When he became a man he joined the group that included Andrew, Peter, James, and John, fishermen from Bethsaida, who were earnestly seeking the promised one from God. All of them identified themselves with the great prophet of righteousness and repentance, John the Baptist, and were baptized by him to repentance in preparation for the new day of the Messiah.

When the Messiah actually came, he chose four fishermen from among John's followers to be his first disciples. Soon he called another, Philip. Evidently Jesus saw in him possibilities of kingdom leadership that would make him useful in the circle of the Twelve. Evidently He knew that the new wine of the Kingdom of God could not be contained in the old skins of Jewish legalism, and he welcomed a man whose name indicated an appreciation of the wider world about him. As the Gospel became universal this man could understand and be useful.

The call of Philip receives only one sentence in the Gospel record, "and he [Jesus] found Philip and said to him, 'Follow me.' " The preparation of heart and mind for the call along with any previous contacts Jesus may have had with him is unrecorded. Thus the call centers attention on the fact "he found Philip." This sets the relationship between God and man in proper perspective, for truly man does not find God but is found by God. Man is the lost sheep, the misplaced coin, the wayward son. God is the shepherd tramping the hill, the woman turning her house upside down, the father rushing down the road to welcome the returning son.

Being found by Jesus, Philip hastened to share with Nathanael what God had revealed to him. "We have found him," he said, "of whom Moses in the law and also the prophets wrote, Jesus of Nazareth, the son of Joseph." For Philip the desire of the ages suddenly became a living experience. For an instant the creature shared with the Creator the timelessness of spiritual reality. He discovered who he was and to whom he belonged.

The four incidents in the Gospels in which Philip is mentioned are recorded by John. He is first mentioned in the story of his call; then in the incident of the feeding of the five thousand; again in the coming of the Greeks who wished to see Jesus; and finally in the discourse of Jesus at the Last Supper.

Two of the incidents involving Philip have caused some Bible students to consider him a dullard, or at least a matter-of-fact individual—the feeding of the five thousand and the Last Supper.

In the first of these two stories five thousand people were crowded about Jesus to see his miracles of healing. Some had come a long journey from the other side of the sea and did not have adequate food to strengthen them for the journey home. Jesus turned to Philip and asked, "How are we to buy bread, so that these people may eat?" Philip made the obvious reply, "We have only forty dollars and that won't buy food for five thousand people." Perhaps this reply does indicate a matter-of-factness about Philip. It could as well represent a generosity that was willing to share every cent the disciples had. Philip may be considered dull for not realizing that Jesus could multiply five barley loaves and two fishes to feed five thousand people. But Philip was not the only dull person, for not one of the Twelve nor of the five thousand had any idea of the miracle they were to observe.

Had we been present some of us might have said, "These people came here of their own accord. Let them get food as best they can." And we might have added in a peevish voice, "It would have been better if they had stayed at home anyway; the Master needs rest and quiet. If we give these people food they will only make a greater nuisance of themselves." We would come off no better than Philip.

A stronger case for Philip's unimaginativeness can be made from the incident at the Last Supper of our Lord. In the Upper Room Jesus said, "Let not your hearts be troubled; believe in God, believe also in me. In my Father's house are many rooms. I go to prepare a room for you. When the room is prepared I will come and take you to my Father. No one can come to the Father except by me, for I am the way, the truth, and the life. If you have seen and known me you have seen and known my Father, also."

Philip said to him, "Lord, show us the Father, and we shall be satisfied."

Jesus answered, "Have I been with you so long and yet you do not know me, Philip? He who has seen me has seen the Father: how can you say 'Show us the Father?' "

With all the teaching of Jesus, all his miraculous deeds, all the sacrifices of the apostles to follow him, it would seem that everyone in this select group would know that Jesus and the Father were one. Philip should have known without having to raise the question.

To admit that Philip had a matter-of-fact side to his nature endears him to many. A literalist is often the most dependable of friends. The most popular of the dwarfs in *Snow White and the Seven Dwarfs* is Dopey. Doubtless everyone is a little "dopey" at times, so it is not surprising to find this tendency to be literal in one of the Twelve. But to think of Philip as simply a dull, matter-of-fact man is to misrepresent him. With the Gospel of John the only source of information about Philip, we need to remember that John is fond of using contrast. Through figures of speech he teaches the truth of spiritual fact by comparison with physical facts: spiritual birth is likened to physical birth; the water of life to water from the well; the bread of life to a common loaf of bread; the Way of Life to a road guide. If Philip is dull in comprehending the full meaning of Jesus' teachings as John records them, then also lacking in imagination were Nicodemus, the woman at the well of Samaria, the other disciples, and the multitude. When such a large group displays the same mentality, we may suspect that we are dealing with a literary device rather than with factual delineation of character, for it soon becomes evident that matter-of-factness is not the most important aspect of his personality.

John's Gospel itself gives some corrective to the picture, for the earliest record of Philip shows him instantly accepting Jesus' call to discipleship, and immediately going to persuade Nathanael. Here Philip is the active man of faith. Human nature is very complex and man is capable of combining within himself contradictory characteristics.

Businessmen, traditionally considered the embodiments of conservatism, are nevertheless frequently investors in gold mines, uranium, oil, or real-estate speculation, sometimes losing large sums of money in the desire for quick gains. Successful businessmen combine venture with caution. All venture in business risks a certain amount of failure, but just as surely all caution risks bankruptcy. Philip combined these opposites.

A legend that goes back to Clement of Alexandria, 200 A.D., says that Philip was the apostle who, when Jesus called him to discipleship, replied, "Lord, let me first go and bury my father." But the response of this reluctant disciple seems in direct contradiction to Philip's prompt acceptance of the Master's call as recorded in John's Gospel. The tradition keeps bobbing up, probably because it makes consistent a mental picture that has grown up about the apostle Philip. Even those who know better constantly yield to the temptation to reduce complex personality to the simplicity of a phrase.

We have other important character data on Philip. He was a man of retiring disposition. In the four incidents recorded of him, three times he is sought out by others. Andrew and his friend sought Jesus, but Jesus "found Philip and said to him, 'Follow me.' " The same fact comes to light in the feeding of the five thousand. When the multitude pressed about him, Jesus sought Philip and asked him, "How are we to buy bread to feed all these people?" Philip knew at once the resources at hand, but he had to be sought out before his opinion was given. When the Greeks came up to worship at the Passover, they "came to Philip" with the request, "Sir, we wish to see Jesus." The initiative again was on the part of others. Apparently Philip had solid worth, but he was not one to push himself forward.

Philip had an affinity for things of great importance. It was a great experience to be called to discipleship. It was a great experience to be present at the feeding of the five thousand but more especially to hear Jesus' words that followed the miracle: "I am the bread of life: he who comes to me shall not hunger and he who believes on me shall never thirst."

When the Greeks came to Philip, saying, "Sir, we wish to see Jesus," they saw far more than they expected, for they saw not only the physical man, Jesus; they saw also his inner struggle of soul. To them he said: "The hour has come for the Son of Man to be glorified . . . unless a grain of wheat falls into the earth and dies, it remains alone; but if it dies, it bears much fruit. He who loves his life loses it, and he who hates his life in this world will keep it for eternal life." This description of the glory of finding life by losing it is followed by an honest revelation of the agony of self-sacrifice. "Now is my soul troubled. And what shall I say? 'Father, save me from this hour'? No, for this purpose I have come to this hour. 'Father, glorify thy name.' "

This conversation with the Greek inquirers contains the same ideas as are expressed in the Gethsemane prayer, affording a glimpse into the heart of the Master, revealing the struggle of the will to live against the demands of self-sacrifice; the temporal versus the timeless; the human as against the Divine. This is the ultimate in human conflict, in which man is divided against himself. The Master knew that he could save his body only by losing his soul. But if he chose to save his soul he must lose his body. The agony of this decision, the depth of insight it reveals into the nature of human life and the demands for spiritual achievement, take us to the ultimate in Christian knowledge. No words have proved adequate to convey the total message of the Cross. Philip sensed this message before the Cross was lifted on the hill of Golgotha.

On another occasion when Philip said, "Lord, show us the Father, and we shall be satisfied" he was echoing the demand of the human heart to see the spiritual clothed in the physical. He was asking for a clear visualization of the relation of Jesus, the Son, to God, the Father. In this he was expressing man's desire to know clearly and precisely, to see directly and plainly, and to have spiritual things expressed with the same definiteness as fish in a net or loaves on the common table. "Show us God." "Let us see the Father." Jesus' reply could be paraphrased as follows: "O Philip, have you been so long a time with me and yet you do not know me! No man sees the Father, yet each act and word that expresses His will makes God known. Philip, can't you understand you have been seeing the Father all along as you lived with me? When you understand this, remember that when I leave you, men hungry for God will come to you with the same request, 'Show us the Father.' Philip, do the works that I do and thus reveal God to others as I have revealed him to you. Truth is not a mystery to be understood, but a life to be lived. Truth is never understood until it is lived." It was Philip's question that made possible this revelation.

A wise teacher in a theological seminary advised his students to select great themes for their sermons. Admittedly the students could not adequately develop the greatest themes, but in the attempt to deal with them both the preacher and his congregation would grow. The limited record of Philip's life excludes him from the list of the major apostles. Yet every time Philip appears he is concerned with great themes: sharing Christ with others; breaking the bread of life; finding God revealed in human life; grasping the meaning of the Cross. This affinity for great themes makes Philip the bearer of important messages for spiritual life.

The Scripture leaves us without information about Philip after the death of our Lord. In 195 A.D. Polycrates, Bishop of Ephesus, writing to Victor, Bishop of Rome, states that "Philip, also one of the 12 apostles, died in Hierapolis, and so did two of his daughters, who had grown old in virginity. And another of his daughters after having passed her life under the influence of the Holy Spirit, was buried in Ephesus."

There is a legend about Philip's death that concerns the conversion of Lady Nicanoia and the opposition of her husband, the Roman proconsul. It is a fantastic tale concerning multitudes being struck dead and then made alive again and Mariamme, Philip's sister, dragged down the street naked but protected from view by a heavenly cloud. The legend ends with the crucifixion of Philip, hung head downward facing Bartholomew, who was likewise being crucified, but through the prayer of Philip was taken down and allowed to live. After his death Philip was wrapped for burial in sheets of Syriac paper and papyrus reeds because he did not wish to be wrapped in linen as was his Lord.

Philip, the tetrarch, was an important man, ruler of Ituraea and builder of Bethsaida Julias, but time has all but blotted out his name. The same passing years have served only to add brighter glory to the apostle who bore the same name. This is the Lord's doing and it is marvelous in our eyes.

NOTE: Philip, Andrew, and Peter were from Bethsaida. Mark indicates that Bethsaida was only a short distance from Capernaum. Luke locates the miracles of the loaves and fishes at Bethsaida, as does the most logical interpretation of Matthew and John. Mark, however, says that after the miracle of the loaves and fishes Jesus and his disciples crossed Lake Galilee to go to Bethsaida. The more conservative scholars solve this difficulty by having two Bethsaidas, the first Bethsaida Julias at the mouth of the Jordan River on Lake Galilee, the second a suburb of Capernaum. Others merely say that Mark in his designation of places and movements is "vague and at times confusing." These scholars point out that save for the problem of harmonizing Gospel records, "there is no evidence of any . . . second Bethsaida." The discussion in this chapter is based on one Bethsaida. Those who wish a fuller discussion of this point can easily find material in standard reference books and commentaries.

7

Nathanael Bartholomew

SAINT BARTHOLOMEW'S DAY August 24

The Collect

O Almighty and everlasting God, who didst give to thine Apostle Bartholomew grace truly to believe and to preach thy Word; Grant, we beseech thee, unto thy Church, to love that Word which He believed, and both to preach and receive the same; through Jesus Christ our Lord. *Amen.*

BARTHOLOMEW IS LISTED AS AN APOSTLE IN THE FIRST three Gospels and in Acts. Aside from these four references there is no mention of him in the New Testament.

Although the Gospel of John does not mention Bartholomew, it does tell of a Nathanael; and there are good reasons for identifying these two as the same person. In the lists of the apostles, Philip and Bartholomew are mentioned together. In John's Gospel, Philip is shown as leading Nathanael to Jesus. In each case a close friendship with Philip is indicated. Moreover Bartholomew is not a name but a patronymic, meaning "son of Tholmai." Even as Peter was called Simon Bar- (son of) Jona, it is possible that Nathanael was called Nathanael Bar- (son of) Tholmai.

In the last chapter of John's Gospel seven men are listed as being present at Jesus' lakeside appearance. Six of these men are known to be apostles. Nathanael is mentioned as the seventh and it seems logical to assume that he also was an apostle. All of those whose call to discipleship is recorded became apostles. If Nathanael were not an apostle, he alone would be an exception to this rule. This identification of Nathanael and Bartholomew cannot be absolutely proved, but it is a reasonable conjecture and on it some information can be found about this disciple of our Lord.

When first mentioned in the Gospel of John, Nathanael was under a fig tree reading the Scripture and quietly meditating. This brief glimpse of a man withdrawn, seeking deeper levels of life through prayer and meditation, gives a clue to his character.

Aloneness, meditation, and prayer are more frequently praised than practiced in the modern world. When not talking with others contemporary man is being talked to by radio, TV, record player, motion picture, telephone, or some other talking machine. One or more of these devices is found in practically every room in the modern home, in most places for public assembly, and even in our private and public vehicles of transportation. Silence is hard to come by today. Yet Arnold J. Toynbee, after exhaustive study of the rise of civilizations, believes that the creative personalities who founded the great civilizations drew their power from the Nathanael-like quality of withdrawal and meditation. Toynbee states:

> Creative personalities, when they are taking the mystic path which is their highest level . . . pass first out of action into ecstasy. . . . The withdrawal makes it possible for the personality to realize powers within himself which might have remained dormant if he had not been released for the time being from his social toils and trammels. Such a withdrawal may be a voluntary action on

his part or it may be forced upon him by circumstances beyond his control; in either case the withdrawal is an opportunity, and perhaps a necessary condition, for the anchorite's transfiguration; "anchorite," in the original Greek, means literally "one who goes apart."

Toynbee illustrates this thesis by reference to Moses on the mountain, Plato in the cave, Jesus in the wilderness, Paul's three years in Arabia, St. Benedict's three years in solitude, Gregory's long period of self-withdrawal, and other like examples.

St. Augustine is another example of a creative personality born in aloneness, for St. Augustine was also alone "under a certain fig tree" when God called him. He records:

I cast myself down I know not how, under a certain fig tree giving full vent to my tears. . . . I sent up these sorrowful words: How long, how long, "tomorrow, and tomorrow?" Why not now? Why not is there this hour an end to my uncleanness? So I was speaking and weeping in the most bitter contrition of my heart, when lo! I heard from a neighboring house a voice, as of boy or girl, I know not, chanting, and oft repeating, "Take up, and read; Take up and read." Instantly my countenance altered. I began to think most intently whether children were wont in any kind of play to sing such words: Nor could I remember ever to have heard the like. So, checking the torrent of my tears, I arose; interpreting it to be no other than a command from God to open the book, and read the first chapter I could find. . . . I seized, opened and in silence read that section on which my eyes first fell: Not in rioting and drunkenness, not in chambering and wantonness, not in strife and envying; but put ye on the Lord Jesus Christ, and make not provision for the flesh in concupiscence. No further would I read; nor need I: for instantly at the end of the sentence by a light as it were of serenity infused into my heart, all the darkness of doubt passed away.

St. Augustine was directed to the life-giving words from the Scripture by a childlike voice, but Nathanael's meditation was broken by the excited voice of his friend, Philip, proclaiming, "we have found him of whom Moses in the law and also the prophets wrote." This announcement was glad news for Nathanael, who, like Simeon of old, was "looking for the consolation of Israel" and the coming of "the Lord's Christ." But joy in the new discovery was lost for Nathanael when Philip continued, ". . . Jesus of Nazareth, the son of Joseph." Now Nathanael was a student of prophecy and he knew that Nazareth was not mentioned by the prophets, nor, for that matter, by any writer in the Hebrew Scriptures. It was not only omitted in Holy Scripture, but apparently it had been overlooked by God, for out of Nazareth had never come a prophet, a poet, a priest, or a ruler. As Nathanael knew, the Scripture plainly said, "and thou Bethlehem, in the land of Judah, art by no means least among the rulers of Judah; for from thee shall come a ruler who will govern my people Israel." So the Messiah could not come out of Nazareth. Nathanael's reply showed disappointment: "Can any good thing come out of Nazareth?"

When the Wright brothers were working on the first airplane, word of their experiment spread about Dayton, Ohio, their home town. A local skeptic summed up sentiment when he declared, "No man will ever fly, and if any man does fly it won't be anybody from Dayton. If any man from Dayton flies, it won't be a Wright brother." The skeptic was wrong on all three counts—a man did fly, he was from Dayton, and he was a Wright brother. Jesus observed, "a prophet has no honor in his own country." It is hard to think of greatness springing from familiar soil.

Philip was a practical man. He did not get into a discussion of prophecy, nor did he try to plead the case for Nazareth. He merely said, "Come and see." A pound of demonstration, Philip knew, was worth a ton of argument. With some misgiving Nathanael yielded to Philip's enthusiasm and went to see Jesus.

Seeing Nathanael approaching, Jesus read his face and his heart, exclaiming, "Behold an Israelite indeed, in whom there is no guile!" So far as we know, Jesus had never seen Nathanael before, yet with one look he knew him altogether. "Here," said Jesus, "is a man who is completely transparent, sincere, honest."

It is not necessary to be a Diogenes, going about with a lantern during the daylight seeking an honest man, to realize that complete sincerity and honesty are virtues rare enough to be worthy of commendation. Most people carry some secrets locked in their hearts and understand the experience of conflicting motives and desires. To be without guile, to have the outer and the inner life in complete unity, and to be absolutely honest is an ideal few would boast having achieved.

Little children come nearest to achieving this virtue. Ask a little child how he gets along with his brother or sister, if he fights, who gets his way most often, or what he thinks of members of the family, and you will find the answers completely truthful. Ask the same questions of almost any other age group and see how difficult it is for them to tell the truth.

An experienced counselor knows that it takes weeks or months of patient listening before he will hear the emotionally disturbed simply and truthfully answer questions about relationships with others. Adults have been so thoroughly conditioned to conceal their true feelings, saying the polite thing, trying not to hurt other people's feelings, that they become confused as to what truth really means. Take the simple situation of meeting your neighbor early in the day and being greeted with a cheery "good morning." The fact may well be that it is not a "good morning" but cold and blustery; yet you would never call into question his description of the day. Instead, you reply, "How are you, this morning?" How surprised you would be if your neighbor answered your question and described how badly he had slept the night before, the condition of his digestion, his headache, his neuralgia, or any other of the disorders that are so common in the early morning. Much communication between people is designed to conceal rather than to reveal the truth. In such matters as friendly greetings everyone understands the situation and no harm is done, but when our casual conversations shade off into deliberate deception and dishonesty, real harm can be done. Jesus said, "Let your communication be 'Yea, yea, and nay, nay.' " This honesty may have been in the mind of Jesus when he said, "Except ye repent and become as little children ye cannot enter the Kingdom of Heaven." Little children are truthful. They, like Nathanael, are without guile.

Hearing himself described as "an Israelite indeed in whom there is no guile," and realizing that Jesus had read his secret thoughts, Nathanael asked in amazement, "How do you know me?" Jesus replied, "Before Philip called you when you were under the fig tree, I saw you." Nathanael was completely overwhelmed. How could Jesus know he had been under the fig tree? How could he know what had gone on between him and Philip? "This man knows not only my heart, but all that I do and think," he said to himself. Fully convinced, he exclaimed, "Master, you are the Son of God. You are the King of Israel."

Jesus accepted this pledge of faith and said, "You shall see greater things than these . . . you will see heaven opened, and the angels of God ascending and descending upon the Son of Man." Four times in the Gospel record, angels came to Jesus: at the Baptism, after his temptations, on the Mount of Transfiguration, and in the Garden of Gethsemane. Certainly, the communication between Jesus and the Father was not limited to these four angelic visions. The angels of God hovered about our Lord when he gave the Sermon on the Mount, when he anointed the eyes of the man born blind, when he said, "Woman, where are thine accusers . . . neither do I accuse thee. . . . Go, sin no more." Indeed, angels were continually ascending and descending upon him. What Jesus was promising was that as Nathanael lived with him he would see more and more of the communion of the Son with the Father and the Father with the Son. It was a wonderful promise whose fulfillment brought great joy to Nathanael. Records of these divine revelations are not available, but in imagination the modern Christian can join Nathanael in his heavenly experiences.

Nathanael came from Cana of Galilee, the town in which Jesus performed his first miracle by turning water into wine at a marriage feast. The record of John seems to indicate that Nathanael was on his way to the wedding when called by Jesus.

Tradition has gone so far as to suggest that he was the bridegroom at the Cana wedding.

Although the importance of private prayer and devotion cannot be overemphasized, John Wesley was correct when he insisted: "There is no such thing as solitary religion." Religion relates us to people and to the world about us. A religion that does not join man to man can never adequately join man to God. The friendship of Philip and Nathanael deepened the religious life of each of them.

In tradition Philip and Bartholomew are still linked together. In Hierapolis of Phrygia (sometimes called the City of the Serpent) these apostles destroyed the serpent worshiped by the people and they healed Nicanoia, the wife of the proconsul. Their activity aroused the proconsul to such fury that he ordered both apostles to be crucified. They were nailed opposite to each other so that each could see the other's suffering. Philip prayed for Bartholomew's release and his prayer was answered. Philip died on the cross and Bartholomew continued alone in the Gospel mission.

After this tragic experience in Hierapolis, tradition says, Bartholomew carried the Gospel to that part of India lying next to Asia. It is here, Eusebius tells us, that several centuries later a converted Stoic philosopher, Pantaenus, discovered Matthew's Gospel in Hebrew, brought to India by Bartholomew. The fact that Matthew's Gospel was not written until after 70 A.D. makes this tradition open to serious question.

Returning from India, as the story goes, Bartholomew died from brutal flaying at the hand of King Astyages of Albanopolis in Armenia. In some medieval art Bartholomew is pictured holding in his hands part of his own flesh. This vivid portrayal of suffering, offensive as it is to modern man, was quite acceptable to the people who placed the pictures in their cathedral windows. From this tradition has come the symbol of the flaying knife to represent this apostle. Many of the traditional stories about Bartholomew, such as the fantastic adventures among the Kurds recorded in the Apocalyptic Gospel of Bartholomew, are unreliable and as unacceptable to modern Christians as they were to Gelasius, Bishop of Rome, who indignantly branded them heresy.

In religious history St. Bartholomew's Day is remembered as the date chosen by Catherine de Medici, August 24, 1572, for the massacre of the Huguenots. At that time one tenth of the population of France was Protestant (Huguenot). Because of personal disagreement with Admiral Coligny, a Huguenot, Catherine wished to do away with them. To achieve this end she persuaded Charles IX to authorize a general massacre of all Huguenot leaders. The massacre went far beyond the taking of the lives of the leaders. It raged in Paris for three weeks and then continued for a like period of time in the provinces. An estimated fifty thousand persons were killed. In celebration of the occasion Pope Gregory sang the Te Deum, ordered bonfires to be lighted, and struck off a medal to keep its memory alive.

To our generation, which accepts the principle of religious freedom, persecution and death for worshiping God in accordance with a man's own conscience seem most horrible. Our temptation is not to compel uniformity in religion but uniformity in other areas of thought and action. Today the struggle of freedom versus conformity is centered in the political and economic field. The last decade has seen books burned, people jailed, and the rights of assembly restricted by a people who pride themselves on believing in the four freedoms. It takes a long time for history to teach the simple lesson that uniformity attained by persecution weakens rather than strengthens a people. St. Bartholomew would disapprove the lack of tolerance in our day as heartily as he would disapprove the bloody massacre by Catherine de Medici in the sixteenth century.

Jesus' description of Nathanael as "an Israelite indeed, in whom there is no guile" shows a disciple who as a young man had a spiritual maturity that would be worthy of praise at the end of life. Not content with this maturity, he went on to "greater things" and saw "heaven opened, and angels ascending and descending upon the Son of Man." There can be little doubt that

Nathanael was an apostle worthy of an honored place among the Twelve chosen by Jesus.

The hymn of William W. How expresses the gratitude each generation feels for Nathanael and for all who like him serve the Lord with fidelity.

> For all the saints, who from their labors rest,
> Who thee by faith before the world confessed,
> Thy Name, O Jesus, be forever blest.
> Alleluia, alleluia!

8 Matthew, the Tax Collector

SAINT MATTHEW'S DAY September 21

The Collect

O Almighty God, who by thy blessed Son didst call Matthew from the receipt of custom to be an Apostle and Evangelist; Grant us grace to forsake all covetous desires, and inordinate love of riches, and to follow the same thy Son Jesus Christ, who liveth and reigneth with thee and the Holy Ghost, one God, world without end. *Amen.*

LEVI SAT AT HIS SEAT OF CUSTOM IN CAPERNAUM COLlecting taxes for Rome. Almost a century previous Rome had taken control of Palestine. Realizing that commerce was the blood of empire and that roads were the arteries through which commerce flowed, the Romans constructed one of the finest systems of roads ever built. One branch of the great road from Babylon came through Capernaum on the way to the Mediterranean and to Rome.

The Romans built these roads by laying a firm foundation of large rocks, covering them with smaller rocks, and then constructing the surface with flat stones fitted closely together and set in cement. Some of these Roman roads were three feet thick and so well laid that portions of them are still in use today. Not until around 1800, when McAdam taught the modern world the importance of drainage and nonporous surfacing, had Europe possessed as good a road system as the one built by the Romans. Over these roads commerce flowed freely and Rome prospered.

As Levi sat at his seat of custom he saw the people of the world pass by: travelers from Mesopotamia, sheiks from the oases of the deserts, artisans from the East, enterprising salesmen from Rome. The colorful apparel of far-off lands brightened the landscape. People with strange languages struggled for methods of communication. Soldiers with flashing armor and bright-colored plume-topped helmets mingled with fine ladies and get-rich-quick adventurers. Levi had an exciting job with endless variety.

Most of the traffic on the road moved on the backs of camels or donkeys, although slaves and hired men often carried burdens and two- or four-wheeled carts were familiar vehicles.

The commerce of the road consisted of jugs from Sidon, baskets from Egypt, veils from Arabia, plates from Babylonia, sandals from Laodicea, shirts from Cilicia, and other skilled handwork in woods and metals. Some nonperishable foods, such as Median beer, Italian wines, Cretan apples, and Bithynian cheese, were exchanged between nations. Local Palestinian exports were largely agricultural: wheat, olive oil, balsam, honey, and figs.

To insure protection from bandits and robbers soldiers patrolled the roads. Thanks to the efficiency of the patrol system, trade was safe from the peril that was so great a barrier to commerce in regions where the protection of the law was not enforced. But roads and soldiers cost money. Hence Levi's responsibility. He was the collector of taxes that paid for the roads and the soldiers, and also for public buildings, offices for the government, markets, town halls, baths, and stadiums. Even the Temple at Jerusalem built by Herod (37 B.C.–4 A.D.) came from taxes collected by men like Levi.

Imperial Rome did not spend tax money for public education

or welfare beyond distribution of food in Rome itself. However Rome did spend—as do modern nations—vast sums for military establishment, roads, public buildings, and government administration. To finance these vast expenditures she utilized duties on imports and exports, taxes on property, land, business, sales, and an income tax of a modest 1 per cent. Almost all the devices modern man uses for taxation, Rome used, plus one that modern states do not have, a "death duty." Perhaps tax experts of today think they have an equivalent in the inheritance taxes.

The importance of Levi's office as tax collector invested him with an authority obvious to everyone. His word was law; men obeyed his orders promptly. Those whose goods passed under his inspection were exceedingly careful to win and to hold his good will. Casual strangers from afar were bound to get the impression that Levi was a successful man, honored and respected in the community. The more observant, however, noted that while people with taxable items showed great respect for Levi, the religious leaders, Scribes and Pharisees, passed by on the other side of the road, carefully avoiding so much as a look in his direction. No one of them ever stopped for a pleasant word or called out a friendly greeting. Small boys, whose actions frequently express the thinking of their elders, threw stones at Levi. The bolder among them spat on his garments and then scampered into the narrow alleys before they could be caught.

The fact was that in spite of the importance of Levi's work he was despised by his fellow countrymen. He levied taxes for a foreign government. Although the country had been occupied by Rome for almost a century, patriotic Jews did not condone the occupation any more than when it had first come to pass. Even the arguments about peace and prosperity did not satisfy those who loved independence. To patriotic men Levi was an enemy agent, a collaborator, a traitor. He continued to sell his nation for personal gain.

To a degree the tax rate was fixed by the tax collector rather than by law. Frequently the privilege of collecting taxes was bought at public auction and to the tax collector went all profits over and above the required tax levy. Because of the obvious injustices the system invited, tax collectors were all considered thieves. Tacitus erected a statue to an honest tax collector, a fact which speaks forcefully of the dishonesty of the usual man in this position. Coupled with the patriotic objection to taxation by a foreign power and resentment at the inequality of taxation was the belief of religious Jews that their nation was a theocracy and that only a God-appointed person had the right to demand tax.

When Levi opened the door to the tax collector's office he probably closed the doors to the homes of his Jewish friends. No respectable person would have him as a guest in his home. His money was not acceptable in the synagogue. His word could not be used in a court of law. He was called a "licensed robber," "wild beast in human shape," and classed with "whoremongers, brothel keepers, parasites, and informers." In the Scriptures tax collectors (publicans) are linked with sinners.

No doubt in the quiet of the night Levi often asked himself if he had made a good bargain. True, he had more money from this tax-collection business, but to his surprise he found that money did not buy everything. Lifelong friends and kindly neighbors snubbed him. Other tax collectors and men who did not adhere to Jewish law, whom he had been forced to choose to replace former friends, did not meet his need for fellowship. Perhaps his wife also felt the estrangement from old friends and old ways. She did not like being shut out from the synagogue guild and the social life of the city just at the time when she could afford to do many things she had always wanted to do. The good clothes she wore meant little if there was no one to admire them. Servants in the house provided leisure that only made her more lonely. She was constantly irritable and nagging. Levi's son was showing symptoms of revolt and misconduct. His daughter could associate only with the limited group of his companions, few of whom Levi wanted for a son-in-law.

In some such discontent Levi turned to the Holy Scriptures. Every leisure hour he poured over the prophets, the law, and the writings as if to prove to himself that he was as deeply loyal as any.

Especially did he study the prophecies about the promise of a Messiah.

John the Baptist was then preaching, "Repent, for the kingdom of heaven is at hand . . . prepare the way of the Lord, make his paths straight." Levi's heart quickened as he realized he was living in the days of fulfilled prophecy. Ruled out of the synagogue, he increased the zeal with which he sought a personal relationship with God and an understanding of the signs of the times. John welcomed publicans and said some harsh things about Scribes and Pharisees. Levi felt encouraged by this attitude to seek more diligently God's plan for his own life.

But before Levi completely adjusted himself to John's preaching, a new and even more vital voice was heard in Capernaum. Jesus of Nazareth began to stir the people by words as remarkable as those of John the Baptist and by deeds far exceeding anything John ever did. In Levi's own city of Capernaum, Jesus cast an unclean spirit out of a man in the synagogue, healed Simon's mother-in-law of a serious fever, and at sundown as the multitudes thronged Simon's door healed many who were sick with various diseases and cast out many demons. He even dared to reach out his hand and place it on a leper, cleansing him of his leprosy. When a paralytic was brought to him, Jesus said, "Your sins are forgiven." The Scribes and Pharisees were scandalized. "It is blasphemy," they cried out, "who can forgive sin but God alone?"

Levi noted that the opposition of the Scribes and Pharisees seemed to increase the popularity of Jesus. The common people heard him gladly and spread his fame through the surrounding region of Galilee. "We never saw anything like this," they said, as they gave God the glory.

Some of these great events Levi may have witnessed with his own eyes; others he knew by hearsay. In his heart he often searched for the meaning of it all. This surely is a man from God, he felt, for no one could do such mighty works unless God were with him. The healing of men's diseases was proof enough of God's power, but the healing of the soul through forgiveness was an even more certain sign of the presence of God. Forgiveness of sins meant much to Levi and as he thought about it he asked himself again and again if there could be a place for him in this new Kingdom of God.

With increasing hope Levi sought out Jesus of Nazareth on every possible occasion. When Jesus performed mighty acts Levi felt himself in the presence of Almighty God. When Jesus spoke, the words seemed intended for him alone. Even in a crowd he had a feeling that Jesus was thinking of him. In all probability Jesus was indeed conscious of Levi's presence and noted his spiritual response. One day while speaking to the multitude Jesus looked Levi straight in the face and gave him a warm and friendly smile. It may well have been the first friendly smile that Levi had received since he began the abominable business of collecting taxes. He did not know the full meaning of that smile, but he knew that in some way the world changed for him. He had no idea what demands Jesus might make of him if he became a follower, but he knew he was ready for any sacrifice. He was prepared for whatever God wanted him to do and was sure that God would soon make known to him his plan.

Levi did not have long to wait. A few days later Jesus passed by his seat of custom. The record says, "Jesus . . . saw a man . . . sitting at the tax office." Where others saw a despised tax collector, Jesus saw a man with hidden hungers, divine desires, and a heart already yielded to the demands of the Kingdom. Jesus said to him, "Follow me." Levi arose and followed him.

The simplicity of the Gospel story conceals the radical nature of Jesus' call of Levi, the tax collector. The respect modern Christians have for Jesus' disciples softens the impact of the disrespect attached to Levi and to his office. To feel the force of Levi's decision as it affected the people of his day, we have constantly to remind ourselves of the popular sentiment against all tax collectors. Moreover, at the time when Jesus called Levi, the Kingdom of God movement was gaining in public approval. A religious revival was in the making. All signs pointed to a movement of national significance. From the point of view of worldly wisdom, calling Levi as an apostle was most unwise. In modern times it would be as if the Community Fund elected as chairman a man just released from prison for embezzling funds from a bank; or the Republican party nominated for Vice-President a well-known Communist; or the visiting Methodist Bishop went home to dinner with the local tavern keeper. "Oil and water are not intended to mix" was the reaction of many. "We could tell Jesus a thing or two about the kind of world we live in," people said. "We may not be so good at forgiving sinners but we have 'know-how' on how to get things done. We could tell him right now that the choice of this disciple does not argue well for the future. There's trouble ahead."

Before the day was over no doubt these hidden thoughts were publicly expressed to the disciples. But Jesus, confronted with this criticism, was not in the least disturbed, for he knew his choice was sound and that God would use Levi for good.

Levi, overjoyed at the call to be a disciple of Jesus, prepared a great feast in honor of the occasion. He invited the only guests who would eat in his house, tax collectors and "sinners," outsiders, men who had failed to keep the Law. Jesus joined in the festal occasion with the invited guests. Levi was eager to have his friends meet Jesus, to know of the new life that had come to him and caused him to forsake old ways.

Apparently, one distinctive mark of those who come into fellowship with Jesus has always been a desire to share their experience with others. This tendency is as marked in the twentieth century as in the first. For example, in Baltimore, where a new jail had been recently built, a pastor interested in improving religious service in the jail was being taken on a tour through the institution by the warden, who remarked, "I get more help out of Alcoholics Anonymous than from any other group that comes to this jail; they come every week and work especially with those who are in jail for drunkenness. The leader of Alcoholics Anonymous has himself been in jail one hundred and ten times for drunkenness. I get a great thrill when I see this man come in here clean shaven, well dressed, anxious to help other alcoholics. I remember how he used to look as an alcoholic on his previous trips."

A fundamental principle of Alcoholics Anonymous is just this point—they must help other people who suffer from the weakness that caused their fall. They must share. When they cease to help other people, they themselves often fall victim to the habit again. No one can help an alcoholic as effectively as the person who has himself been an alcoholic. This need for give and take provides a fundamental fellowship.

Long before Alcoholics Anonymous learned the Christian principle that one must help others if one wishes to help himself, Levi invited his friends to meet Jesus. The record does not tell of the effect of the feast on the guests, but it indicates a change in Levi's life. The man who had been a publican became a disciple of Jesus Christ.

In recognition of this change in Levi's life, possibly at this very feast, Jesus announced that Levi was henceforth to have a new name, Matthew—"Gift of God." Levi accepted the new name gladly, for it signified more than a change of name; it marked a change of life. This was indeed a "Gift of God."

The Scribes and Pharisees did not share the joy of the festive occasion. To them the whole affair was a scandal. Tax collectors and sinners! It was beyond their understanding that a religious teacher like Jesus would be found in such company. They sought out the disciples and asked, "Why does your Master eat with tax collectors and sinners?" The disciples did not know how to answer. But then, the Scribes and Pharisees probably did not want an answer. Rather, they wanted to find fault and to spread dissension among the disciples. Proper people like the Scribes and Pharisees never understand unconventional action regardless of the motivation. The selection of Levi as a disciple merely confirmed their prejudices: "A man is known by the company he keeps." "This man Jesus is misleading the people. He's a wild-eyed fanatic—a sinner himself. No good will come from him!"

Jesus, knowing both the question the Scribes and Pharisees asked his disciples and their inability to answer it, formulated his

"Apology for Loving Sinners." It is one of the most revealing of his statements, disclosing the central motives of his life and thought.

Human need is the first justification for loving sinners cited by Jesus. "Those who are well have no need of a physician," he said, "but those who are sick: I have come not to call the righteous, but sinners to repentance." How hard it is for good people to understand the love of Jesus for the sinful! The miserable of the world gathered about him, and he healed them. The social outcast came and he said, "Neither do I condemn you; go, and do not sin again." Sophisticated modern man, like the Scribes and Pharisees, prefers to gather his robe close to himself to avoid pollution from the masses. Visiting the sick and sinners does not make for his peace of mind.

The Christian Church today, like the individual Christian, also finds it easier to serve the saint than the sinner, the well than the sick. The Church is more at home in Suburbia than in Old Town, in the colonial mansion than in the shack of the sharecropper. Old Town, where live the relief client, the unemployed, the poorly paid, and the lawbreaker, has few churches, and such as it has are inadequately staffed and struggling with small budgets and outdated equipment. Hidden away from Main Street in isolated units neglected and forgotten, people live untouched by the Gospel of Christ. Moreover, rural areas as well as the cities have their overlooked slums. Socially sensitive ministers, who have tried to bring the outcasts into respectable churches, have heard from modern Scribes and Pharisees. The issue raised at the feast of Matthew is by no means dead.

Sixteenth Street, in Washington, D.C., is lined with some of the most beautiful churches in the city. Elder Michaux, a well-known radio free-lancer, recently commented, "God is not in any church on Sixteenth Street." Anyone with spiritual insight would hesitate to say such damning words, yet every person going to a Sixteenth Street church must feel the pull of the neglected slums of our capital city. Unless a Christian is constantly disturbed in his comfortable church and is constantly seeking, like our Lord, to minister to the least and the lost, he is facing the danger of saying, "Lord, Lord!" Only to have the Lord reply, "I never knew you."

In the human body the healing white corpuscles rush to the place where there is a wound or harmful bacteria, concentrating in the place of greatest need. That is as it should be. Physicians are for the sick just as salvation is for sinners. Jesus said, "I am come to seek and to save that which is lost."

Jesus' "Apology for Loving Sinners" cites also the will of God. "Go and learn what this means," Jesus said, quoting from the prophet Hosea, "I desire mercy, and not sacrifice." If the reply is enlarged from words later spoken, Jesus said, "God is not interested in proper observances of ceremony or endless rules that are so extreme that they become burdensome to common life. God wants understanding, friendliness, and sharing of others' needs. God does not add weight to men's burdens. He gives wings to the spirit and a song in the heart. He desires mercy, and not sacrifice."

A young minister in the Church of God recently took up a pastorate in an area near Washington. Finding the membership of his congregation about 50 per cent illiterate, he started a class to teach them to read according to Laubach's method. Serving a like constituency, a young Methodist minister found his parish was being taken over by new $25,000 to $35,000 homes. The young pastor hoped to serve both elements, the low-literacy group and the high-income group. The fact that the situation presented almost insurmountable problems is a serious reflection on our Christianity and on the complacency with which our churches identify Christianity with social status and reduce the Church to a sanctuary for the sanctified. God have mercy on us.

The story of the Prodigal Son is perhaps the most famous of all the wonderful stories told by Jesus. Everybody remembers Jesus' vivid account of the young man who obtained his share of the property and left home to journey into a far country where he squandered his substance in loose living. When a great famine arose the young man was so destitute that he would gladly have fed on food that the swine ate. In this low estate he thought of his father and in repentance arose and returned home to be welcomed with great rejoicing.

Hollywood has filmed this story with emphasis on the loose-living period. Preachers have used it as a parable of the loving God. Others have retold it as the Odyssey of mankind. Jesus used the story to highlight the portrait of the Elder Brother who stayed at home and looked after the farm. To him the father said, "You have all that is mine." All of his father's possessions, all of his father's love, belonged to the Elder Brother, but he lacked his father's understanding and compassion. Lacking compassion, he refused to go into the house to rejoice over the return of his wayward brother, shutting himself out from the music, the dance, the feast. The fellowship of the home, once broken by the departure of the Prodigal, was again broken by the Elder Brother's lack of love. This is Jesus' caricature of the religious leaders of his day. Does it apply to the present time as well?

Near the end of his ministry Jesus severely condemned the current religious leaders. In a series of seven woes recorded in the twenty-third chapter of Matthew, he laid bare the weaknesses that so easily beset organized religious life—rigidity, formalism, externalism, and inhumanity. Jesus' condemnation was not directed only against the religious leadership of his own day. The disturbing truth is that the weaknesses Jesus exposed are all too often present in every generation. Christian leaders would do well to study the parable of the Elder Brother with even greater care than the parable of the Prodigal Son. Good people easily become so good that they cannot mingle with human beings and are hence good for nothing. It is here that every Christian needs constant heart-searching and divine help.

On another occasion Jesus added a third principle to his "Apology for Loving Sinners." At a feast in the home of a Pharisee a woman of shameful past washed his feet with her tears and dried them with the hair of her head. When the Pharisee complained that Jesus would not have allowed this act had he known her past, Jesus said, "Her sins, which are many, are forgiven, for she loved much; but he who is forgiven little, loves little." Sin, tears, love, forgiveness—"proper" people cannot understand these, but Jesus did and gave his fullest blessing to the woman at his feet.

The poet Francis Thompson would have understood the sinful woman. While studying medicine in London, he became the victim of the opium habit. He lost contact with his parents, sold his books, slept in arches or huddled on benches by the Thames. He became a bootblack and was glad to hold a horse's head for a few coppers. In this destitute condition he contracted tuberculosis and hovered between life and death. One who saw him in this sickness described him as "a waif of a man . . . more ragged and unkempt than the average beggar, with no shirt beneath his coat and bare feet in broken shoes." The doctors said he could not live; yet loving hands took hold of him and by the grace of God he did survive. His mind became clear and he wrote what many consider the greatest religious poem in the English language, "The Hound of Heaven." From his own experience he says:

> I fled Him, down the nights and down the days;
> I fled Him, down the arches of the years;
> I fled Him, down the labyrinthine ways
> Of my own mind; and in the midst of tears
> I hid from Him, and under running laughter. . . .
> those strong Feet that followed, followed
> after. . . .
> Deliberate speed, majestic instancy,
> They beat—and a Voice beat
> More instant than the Feet—
> "All things betray thee, who betrayest Me."

After a description of his long wandering, his suffering, and his complete surrender, he hears "That voice . . . round me like a bursting sea." The voice says:

> "How little worthy of any love thou art!
> Whom wilt thou find to love ignoble thee
> Save Me, save only Me?

All which I took from thee, I did but take
Not for thy harms,
But just that thou mightst seek it in My arms.
All which thy child's mistake
Fancies as lost, I have stored for thee at home;
Rise, clasp My hand, and come!"

Halts by me that footfall;
Is my gloom, after all,
Shade of His hand, outstretched caressingly?
"Ah, fondest, blindest, weakest,
I am He whom thou seekest!
Thou dravest love from thee, who dravest Me."

Only great love born out of great sin, great suffering, and great forgiveness could write "The Hound of Heaven." The poem echoes down the corridor of the human heart, for it is the story of Everyman. Great sin, when brought to God with great love, brings great forgiveness. What further apology need our Lord make for his love of sinners?

What kind of a disciple did the tax collector turn out to be? The Scribes and Pharisees were convinced that no good would come from his call, but Jesus shared no such doubt; he welcomed Matthew as a disciple. Weeks later, when after a night in prayer Jesus chose Twelve to be apostles, the list included the name of Matthew. Jesus had found no reason to change his mind about the tax collector.

The name of Matthew is given in the list of the Twelve apostles recorded in the book of Acts. It is thus assured that Matthew remained loyal during Jesus' lifetime and during the trying days of the Crucifixion. Beyond these facts there is no certain knowledge of Matthew. Irenaeus says that he preached the Gospel among the Hebrews. Clement of Alexandria verifies this, stating that fifteen years were spent in this work. Other tradition tells us that Matthew preached in Asiatic Ethopia, south of the Caspian Sea, in Persia, the Kingdom of the Parthians, Macedonia, and Syria.

The uncertainty that envelops the ministry of Matthew also shrouds his death. Some traditions place it in Naddaba in Arabia, others in Ethiopia. Nor is the manner of his death known. Byzantine art pictures Matthew as an aged man dying in bed while an angel beside him swings a censer. The Greek Church has the symbol of fire for Matthew, lending weight to the idea that Matthew died as a martyr by burning. The symbol of a sword is sometimes used, suggesting that Matthew was beheaded. The apostolic shield representing Matthew has on it three purses, a reminder of his days as tax collector. In the Roman Church the Feast of St. Matthew is September 21. In the Greek Church it is November 16.

The first book of the New Testament bears Matthew's name. "When Matthew rose up and followed Jesus the only thing he took with him was his ink and his pen," said Alexander Whyte, "and it is well for us that he did since he made such good use of them."

The First Gospel is the bridge between the Old Testament and the New Testament. Matthew is contantly quoting the Old Testament prophecy and showing how it was fulfilled in Jesus. This fits in with the idea that Matthew made an intensive study of the Scriptures of his people before the call to discipleship. It also lends weight to the tradition that Matthew for fifteen years was a preacher to the Hebrews.

The First Gospel is characterized by careful arrangement of materials and by interest in numbers. The genealogy of Jesus, for example, has three groups of fourteen names each; there are seven parables in Chapter Thirteen, seven woes in Chapter Twenty-three, and ten beatitudes in Chapter Five. This is the kind of thing that would appeal to a bookkeeping tax collector.

Matthew alone tells the parables of the treasure hid in the field and of the pearl of great price. These teachings would appeal to a man who left all to follow the Master. Matthew's Gospel says: "Do not be anxious about your life, what you shall eat or what you shall drink, nor about your body, what you shall put on," and "What will it profit a man, if he gains the whole world and forfeits his life? Or what shall a man give in return for his life?" Also, "It is easier for a camel to go through the eye of a needle than for a rich man to enter the kingdom of God." These records are very personal to the ex-tax collector.

Matthew, alone among the Gospel writers, tells of the visit of the Wise Men to see the baby Jesus. These strangers from afar came seeking him "born king of the Jews." When they found the infant king they opened their treasure and presented to him gifts, gold, frankincense, and myrrh. A fitting story to come from a man who gave all his wealth, all his heart, and all his life to the Master.

The last words in Matthew's Gospel are, "Lo, I am with you always, to the close of the age." The tax collector, once shut out from the congregation of Israel, was never shut out from the fellowship of the Lord Jesus Christ. Christ remained with him "always." "To the close of the age," even for all eternity, the fellowship of Matthew and his Lord will remain unbroken.

NOTE: Scholars are agreed that the apostle Matthew was not the sole author of the Gospel of Matthew as we have it in the New Testament. Papias about 140 A.D. wrote, "Now Matthew collected the oracles in the Hebrew language, and each interpreted them as he was able." It is believed that "the oracles" were quotations from the Old Testament showing that Jesus fulfilled prophecy and was the promised Christ. This minimum authorship is accepted by most scholars. How much more of Matthew is his original contribution is difficult to state since scholars are disagreed on the subject. The fact that Matthew's business had compelled him to keep records would make him more apt to express himself in written language than the apostles whose daily work did not make this demand upon them.

The Gospel of Matthew contains practically all the material in the Gospel of Mark plus many of the teachings of Jesus not recorded in the first written Gospel. There are about two hundred verses in Matthew not found elsewhere in the Gospels. Recognizing that the "view that Matthew the apostle was the author of the gospel that bears his name has in modern times been generally relinquished by scholars," Dr. Edgar J. Goodspeed recently announced his personal opinion that the ex-tax collector is probably its author. The problem of authorship of the Gospels is very complicated and technical. Any standard reference book or commentary on the Bible will give further details to those who wish to refresh their knowledge or to seek out new facts in this area.

The fact that Matthew's name is assigned to the completed Gospel that begins our New Testament is a great honor. The unknown arranger who placed the name of Matthew upon this Gospel thereby showed the veneration his name carried among the early Christians.

9 Doubting Thomas

SAINT THOMAS' DAY December 21

The Collect

Almighty and everliving God, who, for the greater confirmation of the faith, didst suffer thy holy Apostle Thomas to be doubtful in thy Son's resurrection; Grant us so perfectly, and without all doubt, to believe in thy Son Jesus Christ, that our faith in thy sight may never be reproved. Hear us, O Lord, through the same Jesus Christ, to whom, with thee and the Holy Ghost, be all honour and glory, now and for evermore. *Amen.*

WHEN A MAN INSISTS ON PERSONAL VERIFICATION of facts we call him "doubting Thomas." So common is the expression that for many people it has lost its connection with Thomas, the apostle of Jesus. He had been absent when the Risen Lord first appeared to the disciples and so refused to accept their testimony, but insisted, "Unless I see in his hands the print of the nails, and place my finger in the mark of the nails, and place my hand in his side, I will not believe."

Today the demand for unquestioning belief is not as strong as it has been in some periods of history. Tennyson went so far as to suggest:

> There lives more faith in honest doubt,
> Believe me, than in half the creeds.

During the last century the accomplishments of science, which questions all but completely verifiable facts, have given prestige to the scientific method. But in everyday living we quickly grow weary of people who will not mix a little common sense with their demand for verification. It is not intended as a compliment when we call anyone "doubting Thomas."

Epithets, although colorful, can completely distort a person's true character. In one of his political campaigns Winston Churchill called Clement Attlee "a lamb in lamb's clothing." The exaggeration is obvious, yet it is exceedingly difficult to get out of mind once it is heard. Even so, "doubting Thomas" continues to linger in the mind as partial truth, long after it is recognized that Thomas, the doubter, was really one of the most loyal and steadfast apostles among the Twelve.

"It has happened twenty times if it has happened once," writes Thornton B. Penfield, Jr., "that the very person whom I judge with quick disfavor turns out on further acquaintance to be the one to whom I open my heart and who opens his to me. I disliked Thomas at the start. But to live with him in imagination is to replace one's impression of a man who knows all and believes nothing with that of a very human and very courageous spirit, whose example lifts one's soul like music to the light." The experience of Mr. Penfield awaits all who, like him, live with Thomas in imagination.

All the record we have of Thomas, aside from his name in the lists of the apostles, is in the Gospel of John. The King James Version of John's Gospel speaks of "Thomas called Didymus." The Revised Standard Version translates the Greek word *didymos* into English and speaks of "Thomas, called the Twin." There has been an effort to identify one of the Twelve as the twin of Thomas. Some traditions have invented a twin brother and others a twin sister for him. Eusebius, an early historian, says that Thomas' first name was Judas, but that he went by the name "the Twin" to distinguish him from the other disciples by the same name. Like so many facts in Biblical study, we must leave this twin of Thomas completely in the unknown.

The first Biblical record of Thomas is found in the story of Mary, Martha, and Lazarus. The Bethany home of this family was one of the favorite places in which Jesus stopped for rest and refreshment. Each member was very dear to our Lord. One day when Jesus was preaching across the Jordan, Lazarus was taken seriously sick. In great haste the sisters sent for Jesus to come and heal him. When word of Lazarus' sickness reached Jesus, he did not hasten to Bethany, as the sisters had every reason to believe he would. Instead, he deliberately lingered for two days. The apostles, remembering the threat of mob action on their last trip to Jerusalem, believed that Jesus refrained from going to Bethany because of fear of the people. However, at the end of two days Jesus surprised them by announcing that he was departing for Bethany. They protested, "The Jews were but now seeking to stone you, and are you going there again?" Jesus answered, "Lazarus is dead; and for your sakes I am glad that I was not there, so that you may believe. But let us go to him." Thomas then responded, "Let us also go, that we may die with him."

At first glance this response of Thomas seems to reveal an excessive pessimism. Many scholars have drawn just that conclusion, and on the strength of this verse have considered Thomas a melancholiac. One writer applies to Thomas the line from Gray's *Elegy,* "Melancholy marked him for her own"; another quotes *Pilgrim's Progress,* "He was a man of choice spirit but he was always kept very low, and that made his life so burdensome to himself and to others"; and still another says these words of Thomas, "mark a nature prone to despondency, apt to take the darkest view of things. It is the language of despair and vanished hope." Dr. Alexander Whyte, dean of these Bible students sums up their position when he says, "If to say man is to say melancholy, then to say Thomas, who is called Didymus, is to say religious melancholy."

Some of the most creative spirits have been of like temperament. Georgia Harkness, contemporary theologian, has written a book that relates her personal struggle with depression of spirit, *The Dark Night of the Soul,* a phrase coined by St. John of the Cross to describe his own experience. Dr. Harry Emerson Fosdick, perhaps the most influential preacher of this generation, also records his early struggle with melancholy in his autobiography, *The Living of These Days.* In the Scriptures we have expression of this temperament in Job, Jeremiah, parts of Isaiah, and in many Psalms. Dante Alighieri, Thomas Gray, John Milton, Blaise Pascal, Ludwig van Beethoven, Abraham Lincoln, George Frederick Handel, Jonathan Swift, and Thomas Carlyle are a few among many whose creative work was carried on under the darkness of melancholy. If Thomas were a melancholiac he would have plenty of excellent company.

In spite of these opinions, a close look at the words of Thomas and the occasion on which they were spoken makes it far from certain that he was a melancholiac. The message about Lazarus' sickness reached Jesus in early February when he was "across the Jordan," where he had fled to escape the vengeance of his enemies. The preceding September 23, at the Feast of Tabernacles, they "took up stones to throw at him: but Jesus hid himself, and went out of the temple." Eleven weeks later, at the Feast of Dedication on December 8, "the Jews took up stones again to stone him." In other words, Jesus was "across the Jordan" because twice in a little over four months the Jews had sought to take his life. The disciples, remembering this, protested against the return to Bethany, saying, "The Jews were but now seeking to stone you, and are you going there again?" It is against this background that Thomas said: "Let us also go, that we may die with him."

In spite of danger, Jesus returned to Bethany and spoke the word that raised Lazarus from the grave and restored him alive to the fellowship of his home. The marvel of this great miracle temporarily quieted any tendency toward antagonistic action against Jesus and the disciples. But Jesus did not tempt good fortune; rather he "went from there to the country near the wilderness" and avoided open appearance among the Jews. When, two months later, he went to Jerusalem it was to take a Cross. Three gaunt crosses on Golgotha testify that the fears of Thomas were not mere melancholy but stark reality.

It is easy to confuse a realist with a melancholiac, for both see the difficulties in a situation. The realist sees the hazards in a dangerous position, yet is able to think and to act effectively. The melancholiac broods over imaginary evils, is gripped by excessive fear of true peril, and is so paralyzed by real danger that he is unable to act. Thomas showed none of the weaknesses of the melancholiac. He was a realist who saw danger clearly, yet immediately proposed the action the situation demanded.

"Let us also go, that we may die with him." With these words Thomas stepped forward, leading the disciples to life or death as they followed the Master. These heroic words reflect the spirit of Jesus, who shortly thereafter "stedfastly set his face to go to Jerusalem." If Jesus was going to Bethany, even the possibility of death could not deter Thomas from going with him. Step by step with the Master he marched, ready to share fully and completely any suffering that might come. The disciples followed Thomas, who for the moment had become their leader.

The fact that the journey to Bethany did not result in injury to Jesus or the apostles does not in any way detract from the heroism involved in the trip. During the last world war there were experts whose duty it was to de-fuse the unexploded bombs dropped from enemy aircraft. Many of these experts performed their duty without personal injury. Looking back from the safe distance of time, it could be said that they were not heroes because they were unharmed; but everyone knows that in de-fusing unexploded bombs there is the ever-present possibility of injury and death. The danger is not imaginary but real. It is this factor that makes for courage. Even so, the danger Thomas saw was not imagined but real.

Thomas' next word is recorded in the fourteenth chapter of John. The time was the last night of Jesus' earthly life. Gathered with his disciples, our Lord had broken the bread and passed the cup instituting the sacred sacrament, the Lord's Supper or Holy Communion. Jesus, pouring out his heart to prepare the disciples for the shock of his Crucifixion, spoke words which are among the most cherished in the entire Bible.

"Let not your hearts be troubled," said Jesus. "Believe in God, believe also in me. In my Father's house are many rooms; if it were not so, would I have told you that I go to prepare a place for you? And when I go and prepare a place for you, I will come again and will take you to myself, that where I am you may be also. And you know the way where I am going."

Thomas interrupted these comforting words of Jesus with the blunt question: "Lord, we do not know where you are going; how can we know the way?"

Jesus replied, "I am the way, and the truth, and the life; no one comes to the Father, but by me."

Jesus was talking about the way to heaven; Thomas asked for a road map. Jesus spoke of taking "you unto myself"; Thomas inquired, "How can we be taken unto yourself when we don't even know where you are going?"

This is the realist in Thomas. It is the practical mind facing a mystical demand. It is the man who relied on the seen world trying to grope his way into the world of faith. It is the man of common sense confronted with uncommon knowledge. It is the man who mistakenly carries the language and attitude of the dusty road into the chamber of his beloved.

The conflict between the real and the ideal is a universal experience shared even by little children. Thomas would have understood the little four-year-old boy in the beginners' department of a church school. It was the Lenten season and the teacher was preparing the class for Easter. She held a cocoon in her hand and said, "Children, this is a cocoon. In it a big worm is asleep. He has been sleeping a long time. But soon he will wake up and come out of his shell as a beautiful butterfly." The child interrupted: "Where is the butterfly now?" The teacher turned to the pastor for the answer, but the question was far too deep for him. The teacher did her best and promised, "If you will wait a few weeks I'll show you the butterfly." A short time later the cocoon was found broken open and the poor worm exposed to the cold air. The little boy was a realist: he wanted to see the butterfly and he wanted to see it now! He did not understand the meaning of faith or the necessity of time to reveal a beauty that was not at the moment visible. Unintentionally he destroyed the beauty that faith in time's disclosure could reveal.

Common sense says that there are seven thousand stars visible to the naked eye, but the astronomer has counted twenty million stars. Common sense says a desk is very solid wood, but the physicist says the desk is neutrons and protons in rapid motion. If anyone follows science beyond the monkey-wrench and screw-driver stage, he must go beyond common sense into uncommon knowledge.

"It is the absence of anything like material foundation which makes the earth so secure," said Sir Oliver Lodge. "If it [the earth] were based on a pedestal or otherwise solidly supported, we should be anxious as to the stability or duration of the support, and we should have a royal commission sitting on it." As it is, the world floats in air and man has complete confidence in its stability. The realist cries out for rock, but men of faith know that the unseen force that keeps the earth in its orbit is more dependable than rock. Fundamentally, all power is spiritual. In the unseen lies the only security man can ever possess.

Those who have struggled for an answer to ultimate problems like life and death, tears and laughter, separation and union, creation and destiny, knowledge and ignorance, know the conflict that Thomas faced when he inquired for a road map for life.

This generation, which has gone through two world wars as well as an intellectual, spiritual, social, and political revolution, understands fully Thomas' desire for spiritual certainty.

Events of history have compelled modern man to discuss basic issues and to examine the foundations of all his institutions. At this point he can appreciate Thomas, for that is exactly what he was doing when he asked, "How can we know the way?"

In his poem *My Name Is Thomas,* Penfield catches Thomas' spirit of inquiry. He represents Thomas as comparing himself with Peter in this manner:

> As Life
> Made Peter rash, it made me over cool.
> I seldom spoke.
> I had to think a proposition through.
> And Peter's quick, enthusiastic jump
> To optimistic ends would rouse my blood.
> How could he know so surely at the start
> The truth that life reveals but by degrees?
> My colder logic had to prove each step.
> I held that faith was deeper tested so,
> And lent a calmer courage to one's deeds.

There are many who hearing this comparison would be sympathetic to the feelings of Thomas.

Thomas appears again in the story of the Resurrection. On Easter morning, according to the Gospel of John, the risen Lord revealed himself first to Mary Magdalene. In the evening of Easter Day Jesus appeared to the disciples as they gathered in a room, "the doors being shut . . . for fear of the Jews." Thomas, for some reason, was not present when Jesus appeared to the others. When told of the Lord's appearance he doubted and said, "Unless I see in his hands the print of the nails, and place my finger in the mark of the nails, and place my hand in his side, I will not believe."

Eight days later, the disciples were again gathered, Thomas with them. The doors were shut, but Jesus came and stood among them and said, "Peace be with you." He then approached Thomas and said, "Put your finger here, and see my hands; and put out your hand, and place it in my side; do not be faithless but believing." Thomas answered, "My Lord and my God!"

Jesus replied, "Have you believed because you have seen me? Blessed are those who have not seen and yet believe."

In John's Gospel story the doubt of Thomas stands in sharp contrast to the faith of the apostles. But our judgment of Thomas is somewhat softened when the other Gospels are read, for although they do not record Thomas' doubt they indicate a common skepticism in all the apostles. In Mark's Gospel Jesus "appeared first to Mary Magdalene, from whom he had cast out seven demons. She went and told those who had been with him, as they mourned and wept. But when they heard that he was alive and had been seen by her, *they would not believe it.*" Later Jesus appeared to two of them as they were walking into the country, and they hastened to tell the other apostles. But in spite of the fact that these were the second witnesses to the Resurrection, *"they did not believe them."* When Jesus made a third appearance to the eleven disciples as they sat at table, "he upbraided them for their unbelief and hardness of heart, because they had not believed those who saw him after he had risen." The Gospel of Luke presents a similar picture of unbelief on the part of all the apostles. When the women who had been at the tomb told the apostles of the appearance of the Risen Lord, it "seemed to them an idle tale, and they did not believe them." The records of Mark and of Luke indicate that not one of the apostles believed until he personally had seen the Lord. According to the record of John, it was the misfortune of Thomas that he was absent when the Lord appeared to the others, so that his doubt stood apart from the faith of the ten who had seen him.

It is true that Thomas, when he asked to put his finger in the nail print in the hands of Jesus and to thrust his hand in his side, demanded a proof more physical than that asked by any of the other apostles. However, when Jesus appeared to Thomas and asked him to examine his wounds, Thomas did not accept the offer. He might doubt the word of his fellow apostles but he did not doubt his Lord. In the presence of his Christ he believed as promptly and as completely as had the other apostles. Falling prostrate at Jesus' feet, Thomas exclaimed, "My Lord and my God."

Renan, the French skeptic, said, "We owe the resurrection story to Mary Magdalene, a highly emotional woman." Fortunately, we also have the Resurrection story as experienced by Thomas, a highly intelligent, practical-minded man, who demanded the most rigid evidence as the foundation for his faith. Chrysostom, the Church Father, said, "Thomas doubted that we might have faith."

In Jesus' words to Thomas, "Have you believed because you have seen me? Blessed are those who have not seen and yet believe," we have Jesus' final Beatitude, "Blessed are those who have not seen and yet believe." All who believe in the Risen Lord are truly blessed—blessed because immortal life becomes real, blessed because all life takes on infinite value, blessed because they have fellowship with him beside the open tomb, on the Emmaus Road, in the Upper Room, and to the uttermost parts of the earth.

There is an ancient tradition that Thomas carried the Gospel to India. *The Acts of Saint Thomas the Apostle to India,* a manuscript that goes back to the second or third century, is the oldest written record in support of this tradition.

In *The Acts of Saint Thomas* the apostles are shown as dividing the world among themselves for evangelistic activity. When Thomas was assigned India, he protested, "I cannot go there because of the fatigue of the body on the journey, for I am a Hebrew." Jesus then appeared to Thomas, urging him to go to India, but he continued to resist, saying, "I would that Thou wouldst send me into another country, for unto the country of India I cannot go."

It was then that our Lord showed himself to Abbanes, a merchant from India, and sold Thomas to him as a slave. Thomas, recognizing himself as Jesus' slave, yielded and thus came to India as a slave of Abbanes. When the merchant arrived in India he took Thomas to King Gondaforus. The king inquired of

Thomas his skills and the apostle replied, "I am a carpenter and a stonemason." The king asked, "What canst thou make in wood and what in stone?" The apostle said, "In wood, ploughs, yokes, measures, wheels, whips, oars, and steering poles; in stone, statues and houses and royal palaces." The king was pleased with Thomas and authorized him to build a royal palace.

The apostle selected the site for the palace and "took a reed and measured the ground, and marked out the dimensions of the palace, and the position of the foundations, and the site of the large hall. He made the site of the building to face the east whence cometh the light of the sun, and its windows to face west whence cometh the wind; and the doors of the bakehouse faced the south, and by the side flowed a good stream of water." The king was very pleased and commended the apostle, "Verily thou art a cunning handicraftsman, and it is fitting that thou art in the king's service." He gave Thomas much gold and silver to construct the palace.

When the allotted time for construction had passed, the king came to see his palace. The people nearby told the astonished king, "He hath builded neither a palace nor anything else," and they added, "He hath done nothing except go about the city, and through the region round about it, and what thou didst give him and all that he himself had he hath given to the poor and needy. He hath taught the people a new God, and healed the sick and cast out devils, and performed many wonderful things. We thought that he was a sorcerer, but the things which came from his hands are mercy, grace, and healing; and the humility and wisdom which he showeth through his Faith make us believe that he is indeed an apostle of the God whom he preacheth, and he fasteth and prayeth always. His food is bread alone, his drink is water, his apparel, both summer and winter, is a single garment. He taketh nothing from any man, and whatsoever he hath he giveth unto others."

The king had Thomas brought to him and demanded, "Hast thou built the Palace for me?"

"Yea, I have built it," said Thomas.

"When can we go and see it?" asked the king.

"Thou canst not go to see it now, but only when thou hast departed from this world wilt thou be able to see it."

King Gondaforus, exceeding wroth, cast Thomas into prison. As he pondered the method by which he would take Thomas' life, Godon, his brother, died. In heaven Godon saw a beautiful palace that he desired for his own. Upon inquiry he found it was King Gondoforus' palace. Godon asked permission to return to his brother to persuade him to sell the palace to him.

Godon returned and made his request of Gondaforus, suggesting that Thomas was still alive and could build another palace for Gondaforus for his heavenly home. When the king heard this he brought Thomas from prison, asked his forgiveness, and humbly gave his heart to God.

Until a few decades ago no record existed of a king named Gondaforus and this story was considered entirely legendary. But recent excavations have established that a king by the name of Gondaforus did reign in North India during the time Thomas might have lived there. Coins and inscriptions have been unearthed bearing Gondaforus' name. This leaves to be explained the presence of Thomas in North India when the Christians who bear his name seem always to have centered in South India. Dr. J. N. Farquhar explains this by saying that Thomas remained in North India until war destroyed Gondaforus and his kingdom, and then he went to South India. Hazel E. Foster thinks that "this reconstruction of what may have happened has as good historical underpinnings as have the various stories regarding the origin of other ancient churches."

Bishop Philipose Mar Chrysostom of Kottayam, a delegate to the World Council of Churches, expressed the opinion of the Indian Christians when in September, 1954, he said to a small group in Washington, D.C.: "Yes, I feel sure that Saint Thomas founded our church. Surely Thomas would have preached the Gospel somewhere. Since India is the only country that claims him, he must have preached in India and founded the Mar Thoma Church."

In 1952 the Syrian Christians celebrated the 1900th anniversary of the arrival of Thomas in their country. In connection with this celebration the World Council of Churches held three important meetings. The Study Committee and the Central Committee met at Lucknow and the World Council of Christian Youth met at Kottayam.

Aside from the tradition that Thomas founded the Church in India little is known of the early history of this ancient Syrian Church. Unfortunately when the Portuguese arrived in India they destroyed the church records, hoping thereby to destroy what they considered a heretical brand of Christianity. Under the impact of Portuguese influence the Church in India embraced Roman Catholicism. Between the years 1599 and 1653 the Roman Catholic influence was in complete control. Evidently this control did not completely destroy the love of old ways and old friends. Many remembered with longing the centuries when the Church had received its bishops from the Nestorian Patriarch of Edessa (Babylon). When word of the lingering desire for his ecclesiastical supervision reached the Patriarch of Edessa, he sent a bishop to the Church in India. But the bishop never arrived. Word spread among the people that Roman Catholic leaders had killed him. Whereupon 200,000 families left the Catholic Church, leaving only 400 families within her fold. Missionary efforts were promptly undertaken that succeeded in winning back 100,000 to the Catholic faith. Today the Uniat Roman Syrian Church, as the Roman Catholics there are called, has grown to be the most numerous group in Travancore-Cochin.

In the nineteenth century the Protestant Syrian Church was divided by internal disputes over property rights. The Jacobite or Orthodox Syrian Church, although the larger group, with 450,000 members, continues to suffer from the controversy over property rights and the powers of bishops. In spite of these troubles it carries on aggressive educational, youth, and missionary activities. The other branch, the Mar Thoma Church, with only 150,000 members, is noted for evangelism and social zeal. Beginning in 1889 without any property, it has developed a vigorous program and become the leading Syrian Church, standing high among the world churches in Christian zeal and thought. Both the Mar Thoma Syrian and the Orthodox Syrian Christian churches are members of the World Council of Churches. The growing influence of the Mar Thoma Church was dramatized when in 1954 the World Council of Churches elected Archbishop Mar Thoma Juhanon, Metropolitan of the Mar Thoma Church, as one of its six presidents.

Thomas, tradition says, died a martyr's death on a mountain now called Mount Thomas in Mylopur, a suburb of Madras. His death was accomplished by piercing with a lance. A shrine erected by the Portuguese marks the sacred site.

A hymn of praise recorded in *The Acts of Thomas* expresses the great honor given the church by the Syrian Christians:

> The church is she in whom is the splendor of royalty. She is pleasant of aspect and lovely. Beautiful is she to him that looketh upon her. Her garments are like unto flowers of every kind, and the odor thereof cometh forth and anointeth the head. . . . Truth is upon her head, and joy with her feet.

The Acts of Thomas gives a description of the all-night service used by Thomas to receive Gondaforus into the Christian Church:

> They brought oil and lighted many lamps, for it was night. Then the Apostle rose up, and prayed over them with his voice, saying, "Peace be unto you, O my brethren." Now they heard the voice only, but they did not see his form, for as yet they had not received baptism, and the Apostle took the oil and poured it over their heads, and recited prayers over them, and he answered and said,
>
> "Let the name of Christ, which is over all things, come!
> Let the name which is holy, and exalted, and perfect in mercy, come!
> Let thy mercy come!
> Let that which is a hidden mystery come!
> Let the mother of the seven mansions come, and let thy rest be in the eighth habitation.

Let the intercession of Wisdom, and Counsel, and
Understanding come and unite itself with
these young men!
Let the Holy Spirit come and cleanse their hearts
and veins!"

And he prayed over them in the name of the Father, and of the Son, and of the Holy Ghost. And when the exorcisms had been said a young man appeared unto them, and He held a lighted lamp in His hand, and straightway all the other lamps died down, and flickered and became extinguished. Then the Apostle said unto the Lord,

"O Thou who art Almighty, we cannot bear the light which Thou hast revealed unto us, for Thy grace is more mighty than ours."

And when the dawn came and it was morning, the Apostle gave them the Bread of Union, and they stood up in thanksgiving to Christ, and rejoiced and were glad.

This inspired drama of the reception of Gondaforus into the Church probably had assistance from spirit-filled men who used the service after the death of Thomas. Even in cold print the dramatic action of passing from darkness to dawn is deeply moving. The effect upon those experiencing it must have been profound.

Thomas, alone among the Twelve, has a Church that bears his name with a history dating back to the earliest days of the Christian movement. The Church he founded lived for centuries in isolation from its Christian brothers, a little island of lovers of the Lord in a hostile world. For fidelity over a long period of time under conditions demanding unusual courage, no group exceeds the Christians of India.

Thomas, commonly called the "Doubter," was "a very human and very courageous spirit, whose example lifts my soul like music to the light." Like the members of the Church that bears his name, he is best characterized as a man of fidelity, courage, and faith.

10 James, the Son of Alphaeus

SAINT JAMES' DAY May 1

The Collect

O Almighty God, whom truly to know is everlasting life; Grant us perfectly to know thy Son Jesus Christ to be the way, the truth, and the life; that, following the steps of thy holy Apostles, Saint Philip and Saint James, we may stedfastly walk in the way that leadeth to eternal life; through the same thy Son Jesus Christ our Lord. *Amen.*

TWO OF THE APOSTLES BORE THE SAME NAME. JAMES, the son of Alphaeus, ninth in the list of the apostles given in the Gospel of Matthew, is to be distinguished from James, brother of John, the first apostolic martyr. A third James prominent in the New Testament is the brother of our Lord, who is almost unmentioned in the Gospels but emerges as an acknowledged leader in the early Church.

The mother of James, son of Alphaeus, was one of the Marys who stood by the Cross when Jesus was crucified. Her presence there suggests the possibility that she was one of the group of unnamed women who went to anoint the body of Jesus on Easter morning. Certainly James had the gift of a godly mother.

The Book of Common Prayer credits this James with the authorship of the Epistle of James, but most scholars reject this designation. If the work could be considered his, it would be most helpful as an aid to our knowledge of him. However, we do know that James, the son of Alphaeus, was present with the other apostles on the day of Pentecost.

Confusion arises when one tries accurately to identify his mother. As in the case of the mother of James, the first apostolic martyr, the names of the women gathered at the Cross give the only clues. Mark mentions that there were around the Cross "Mary Magdalene, and Mary mother of James the younger and of Joses, and Salome." John lists the group as "the mother of Jesus and his mother's sister, Mary wife of Clopas, and Mary Magdalene." If John meant to identify the sister of Jesus' mother as the Mary who was the wife of Clopas and if this is the same Mary mentioned in Mark's Gospel as James' mother, then the mother of James is the sister of Mary, the mother of our Lord. This line of reasoning gives two names for the father of James, Alphaeus and Clopas—Alphaeus being his Greek and Clopas his Aramaic name. Against this identification that makes James the cousin of Jesus can be pointed out the improbability of two sisters bearing the same name and the lack of sustaining evidence to identify the wife of Clopas either as Mary's sister or as the mother of James. It seems somewhat more likely that Salome, mother of James and John, was the sister of Jesus' mother.

The fathers of both Matthew and James were named Alphaeus. This has led some students to conclude that James and Matthew were brothers. The Gospels clearly state that Peter and Andrew, and also James and John, were brothers, but they make no such statement about Matthew and James. The lack of direct statement in the Gospels making the men brothers seems to indicate that this relationship did not exist. Silence on the subject, however, is not proof; it is possible to accept the idea of blood relationship between Matthew and James.

In the King James Version, Mark's list of the persons about the Cross refers to James as "the less." The Revised Standard Version translates this "the younger," but long usage has fixed upon James the characterization of the earlier version and he is usually identified as James the Less.

This designation "the less" opens the speculation that James was small of stature. While the small of stature sometimes develop an aggressive spirit to compensate for lack of physical size, there is abundant evidence to indicate that smallness in body does not indicate smallness in ability. Among the great military leaders who were small in stature are Alexander the Great, Napoleon, Simon Bolívar, and Commodore John Paul Jones. Great writers who were physically small include Aesop, Cicero, John Milton, Alexander Pope, Isaac Watts, Shelley, Keats, and Victor Hugo. The American statesmen Alexander Hamilton, Aaron Burr, and Alexander H. Stephens were small men. John Wesley was only slightly over five feet tall and Raphael, Sir Isaac Newton, John Jacob Astor, and Steinmetz measured about the same. Beloved Queen Victoria was even shorter. In spite of such a noble company it is doubtful if any would take pride in the designation "the less." James probably preferred to be called "James, son of Alphaeus"; yet the title "the less" sticks to him.

The family of James, son of Alphaeus, was united in love for Jesus Christ. The fact that Mary, his mother, was one of the faithful at the Cross, sharing the sorrow of the mother of Jesus and a few other women, indicates a commitment to the Lord that places her in the inner circle of women who followed him. The record indicates that she was also the mother of Joses. The mention of Joses along with his apostolic brother is probably due to the fact that the readers of the Gospel would remember him as part of the Christian fellowship. Unless Joses was a fellow Christian there seems little reason to include his name at this crucial point. If Joses was a Christian, then it is probable that the entire family—the parents, Mary and Alphaeus, as well as the two sons—were united in love of Jesus Christ. Based on this reasoning, the family of James, like the Bethany family of Lazarus, Mary, and Martha, became one of the first Christian families. Great blessings have been bequeathed to the world through families whose common bond is loyalty to Jesus Christ.

A query in the Book of Discipline prepared by the Society of Friends characterizes the ideal Christian home. "Are you endeavoring to make your home a place of friendliness, refreshment and peace, where God becomes real to all who dwell there and all who visit it?"

The Quaker philosopher, Rufus Jones, lived in a home that was governed by the spirit of this inquiry. He says:

> While I was too young to have any religion of my own, I had come to a home where religion kept its fires always burning. We had very few "things," but were rich in invisible wealth. I was not "christened" in a church, but I was sprinkled from morning until night with the dew of religion We never ate a meal which did not begin with a hush of thanksgiving, we never began a day without a "family gathering" at which mother read a chapter of the Bible, after which there would follow a weighty silence. These silences, during which all the children of the family were hushed with a kind of awe, were very important features of my spiritual development. There was work inside and outside the house waiting to be done, and yet we sat there hushed and quiet, doing nothing. I very quickly discovered that something real was taking place. We were feeling our way down to that place from which living words come, and very often they did come. Someone would bow and talk to God so simply and quietly that he never seemed far away. . . . My first steps in religion were thus acted. It was a religion which we did together.

In contrast stands this autobiographical note from a modern novelist:

> As far back as I can remember my home was a place of turbulent unhappiness. I was always ashamed to invite my friends in because I never knew what kind of scene they might encounter. When I was a little tot, I remember running after my mother down the street, begging her to come home again, for after her violent tirades against my father she would threaten to leave for ever. . . . Looking back upon my home environment, I can account for much of

my morose outlook on life, and the black moods that sometimes almost overpower me. It explains how difficult it is for me to be socially at ease. I am nervous and fidgety and have little self-confidence. The example of marriage that I have had before me all my life has made me horribly fearful that I, too, may make a terrible mistake if I marry. Yet I want to marry—and have a happy husband and children.

More than most people realize happiness or unhappiness in life goes back to the "friendliness, refreshment and peace" of the family.

Friendliness within the family, like friendliness elsewhere, demands time and effort. Simply because a group is related by blood and occupies a common dwelling does not mean that an understanding, friendly spirit will automatically develop. In the home everybody is so busy about his or her major concerns that time for friendliness and fellowship is easily neglected. A few years ago a mother, father, and their eight-year-old son had planned a summer vacation at the seashore, which was the major theme of the family conversation for weeks. Expectation was at a high pitch when just before the vacation the father was put out of work by a strike, causing the vacation to be canceled. Instead of going to the seashore the entire family went to a nearby field to pick blackberries. After the day's outing the youngster said, "I am glad we didn't go to the ocean. We've had a good time together, and look at all the berries we've picked!" Togetherness, time spent enjoying each other, is all-important. Whether this happens in the open field or at the ocean is of small consequence.

Few fathers have had more joy in fellowship with their sons than Theodore Roosevelt. While carrying the heavy responsibilities of President of the United States, he wrote the following letter:

THE WHITE HOUSE
Nov. 15—1903

DEAR KERMIT:

Mother has gone off for nine days, and as usual I am acting as vice-mother. Archie and Quentin are really too cunning for anything. Each night I spend about three-quarters of an hour reading to them. I first of all read some books like Algonquin Indian Tales, or the poetry of Scott or Macaulay. Once I read them Jim Bludsoe, which perfectly enthralled them and made Quentin ask me at least 100 questions, including one as to whether the colored boy did not find sitting on the safety valve hot. I have also been reading them each evening from the Bible. It has been the story of Saul, David, and Jonathan. They have been so interested that several times I have had to read them more than one chapter. Then each says his prayers and repeats the hymn he is learning. Quentin usually jigging solemnly up and down while he repeats it. Each finally got one hymn perfect, whereupon, in accordance with previous instructions from mother, I presented each with a 5¢ piece.

The modern parent exclaims, "There is not time for things like that today." Is it really true that Mr. and Mrs. Average Citizen are more busy than Theodore Roosevelt, President of the United States? Rather than a lack of time is it not a matter of letting lesser things take the place that should be occupied by family fellowship?

Friendliness in the home does not preclude conflict. Children of all ages get on their parents' nerves and, as every child knows, parents are often out of date and unreasonable. Thirty-five families, above average in understanding of human problems, were asked to keep a ten-day record of the number of times problems presented themselves and the frequency of times of irritation. They reported a total of 56 problems and 859 periods of irritation. From this report the home appears more a place of strife than a place of peace. Minor irritation, however, is no barrier to true peace. The home is the workshop where members of a family learn to live and let live, to refuse to build little tensions into major crises, and to enjoy each other in spite of the obvious clashes in daily life.

Reversing the usual procedure of giving family advice to parents, the Prudential Life Insurance Company has issued a bulletin entitled *The Care and Feeding of Parents.*

Parents are nice, rather hard to understand, but—on the whole

—very nice. Inasmuch as they are so, it is a wise child who handles them properly—with gentleness and understanding, for it is only with such care that they thrive.

They will fret when we stay out late. It's one of the chief characteristics of genus parentis. So, a return home at a reasonable hour by teen-agers is one of the best remedies in the world for parents' main occupational disease—nervous collapse from worry.

You may find, however, even when this greatest of hazards to parents' health is eliminated, that they tend to become emotionally upset by such things as the slamming of doors, the heavy tread of jiving feet, or the swoony strains of a record played 15 or 16 times. Lengthy phone conversations on the part of offspring are dangerous too. The male parent, especially, is apt to come to a slow boil at about 20 minutes of phone chatter, and then blow his lid. All these things are to be avoided, if one wishes to preserve the well-being of the older generation.

Parents are to be pampered, spoiled, and—above all—treated as human beings. They love it.

And remember, there are only two to a customer.

The modern home exists in the world of record players, telephones, and TV sets. Yet in spite of new devices the human elements that enter into a family are fundamentally the same as in the past. The home has always sheltered wiggly two-year-olds, self-assertive first-graders, terrible teen-agers, love-stricken adolescents, and parents who refuse to catch the spirit of the times. In spite of the inherent clash between age groups, people find their greatest happiness in good homes.

James, the son of Alphaeus, was prepared for apostleship by living in a good home. Likewise in countless homes today "friendliness, refreshment and peace" prevail and "God becomes real to all who dwell there." From such homes come modern apostles who will, like James, hear the call of the Master and carry the Gospel to the world.

Inasmuch as there are three persons in the New Testament named James, it is not surprising that they should be confused one with the other. In the fourth century Jerome identified James, the son of Alphaeus, with James, the brother of our Lord.

He achieved this ingenious identification by changing all those listed by Matthew as brothers of Jesus to cousins of Jesus. This interpretation, commonly accepted by the Roman Catholic Church, is welcomed by it partly because of the reluctance of a people worshiping the Virgin Mary to admit that Mary could have been the mother of six children in addition to Jesus. There is no Scripture to sustain Jerome's identification of James, son of Alphaeus, with the brother of our Lord, who was the leader of the Jerusalem Church. Indeed, John distinctly states that "his brothers did not believe in him," and Paul credits the change in the attitude of James toward his brother Jesus to a Resurrection appearance of our Lord. Scholars deny the linguistic basis of Jerome's identification, which rests upon the translation of the word "brother" as "cousin."

Jerome's confusion carries over into the legendary material on the subject. The Jameses are used interchangeably. There is no way to untangle the mixed identity any more than there is a way to establish authenticity in the incidents recorded.

According to the report of Hegesippus (169 A.D.) James lived the life of a Nazarene before and after becoming an apostle of Jesus Christ. As a member of this order he drank no wine or other strong drink, ate no meat except the Paschal Lamb, never shaved or cut his hair, and never took a bath. The last-named virtue will not enhance his appeal to modern men, many of whom care little for godliness but are extremely conscious of cleanliness. James wore no clothes except a single linen garment which also carefully avoided cleansing water. He spent so much time in prayer that his knees became hardened like the hoof of a camel.

These virtues, which sound more like the early days of monasticism than the first century of the Christian Church, earned for James the title of James the Just. So righteous was his life that he alone of the Christians was allowed to go into the Holy of Holies, and Jews as well as Christians strove to touch the hem of his garment as he passed in the street.

The Golden Legend, a seven-volume compilation of the lives of the saints arranged by Jacobus de Voragine, Archbishop of

Genoa, in 1275 A.D., relates that James resembled Jesus Christ so much in body, visage, and manner that it was difficult to distinguish one from the other. The kiss of Judas in the Garden of Gethsemane, according to this tradition, was necessary to make sure that Jesus, and not James, was taken prisoner. On the basis of this story James is usually pictured in ancient Christian art as beautiful of countenance. His handsome features, full of spiritual and intellectual beauty, make him easily recognizable in early portraits of the Twelve.

The legend continues that James, the son of Alphaeus, was so stricken with grief at his Master's death that he vowed he would eat nothing until he saw Jesus again in the flesh. Fulfilling this vow, he grew weaker and weaker. As the days passed the apostles tried to prevail upon him to eat, but he resisted all their efforts. Knowing of the fast, Christ appeared to James before appearing to the others and said, "Bring a table and bread, that we may eat together." When the table was brought and bread placed upon it, the Risen Lord broke the bread into two equal parts and gave half to James, saying, "My brother, eat my bread, for the Son of Man is risen from among them that sleep." So James, who had taken no food since Jesus gave him bread and wine in the upper room, took bread again from the hand of the Risen Lord and broke his fast.

Hegesippus tells the story that James, son of Alphaeus, as an aged man was condemned to death by Annas, the High Priest, on the accusation of breaking the law. He was taken directly from the judgment hall to the battlements of the Temple. Here he was given the chance to save his life on condition that he would renounce his Christ. Instead of renouncing Christ, James cried in a loud voice that Jesus was the Son of God seated on the right hand of God and that he would come on clouds of heaven to judge the world. Enraged at his testimony, the priests cast him down from the battlements. Surviving this fall, James struggled to his knees in prayer. Bystanders threw stones at him while he prayed for their forgiveness. A fuller standing by with a club ended James' life by a blow on his head. His body was sawn asunder by his persecutors before he was buried. The saw and the fuller's club are thus frequent emblems used to depict this apostle of our Lord. In the Netherlands a bow like the instruments used in chopping wool is a frequent symbol for James, son of Alphaeus, denoting that he was the patron saint of hatters and weavers.

Josephus declares that the murder of a man as saintly as James was one of the reasons God destroyed the city of Jerusalem. Remembering the home from which James came, it is not surprising to find him undergirded with virtue. A good life would be expected from a man whose mother stood at the Cross and whose father and brother shared the Christian fellowship. From the earliest reference to his discipleship until the tradition of his final martyrdom, James was a faithful apostle of Jesus Christ.

11 Simon, the Zealot

SAINT SIMON'S DAY October 28

The Collect

O Almighty God, who hast built thy Church upon the foundation of the Apostles and Prophets, Jesus Christ himself being the head corner-stone; Grant us so to be joined together in unity of spirit by their doctrine, that we may be made an holy temple acceptable unto thee; through the same Jesus Christ our Lord. *Amen.*

SIMON, THE ZEALOT, IS NOT MENTIONED IN THE SCRIPtures save in the lists of the apostles' names. Two of the lists record his name as Simon Zealot and the others call him Simon the Canaanaean. Canaanaean, scholars say, is the Greek equivalent of the Aramaic word zealot.

The Zealots were ultrapatriotic, intensely religious people bent upon restoring divine rule in Israel. The Zealot movement had its beginning in the rebellion of Judas of Gamala in the year 7 A.D. The immediate cause of the revolt was the taking of a census of persons and property to serve as the basis of a 10 per cent tax on grain and a 20 per cent tax on wine and fruit. From ancient times the Temple had exacted a tithe for the religious life of the nation, so when Quirinus ordered a census for the purpose of collecting a tithe on grain and a double tithe on wine and fruit the Zealots considered the tax to be levied in opposition to the Temple tax and as a blow against religion.

Previous Roman administrators, knowing local sentiment, had avoided similarity to the Temple tithe, so that taxes in the past had consisted largely of tolls, house tax, excise, market tax, head tax, salt tax, crown tax, and custom duties. In most of the Empire, however, direct percentage tax on crops was the general practice. Quirinus considered the direct percentage tax more equitable, cheaper to collect, and therefore in the interest of efficiency and general well-being. From his point of view, the opposition to the tax on religious grounds was irrelevant and senseless.

The Zealots, like the Liberty Boys and Minutemen who fought the battles of Lexington and Concord, were aroused to action by a tax, but fundamentally they were dealing with deeper and more complex problems. Also, like the Liberty Boys and Minutemen, they were involved in the struggle of a colonial power for the right of self-government. They raised the banner of freedom and gave the battle cry "For God and Country." They envisaged Israel as a theocracy, a nation ruled by God. When the Zealots fought for freedom, they fought that God's nation might be governed by God-appointed priests and kings.

The twentieth century has seen 660,000,000 people, one fourth of the world's population, win self-government. Twentieth-century man has heard again the ancient arguments for and against colonialism. Imperial powers have always justified colonialism by the good it achieves for the colonies. So with Rome. She could boast excellent roads, enforcement of world peace through repression of local wars, vast public works in every country, and stimulation of world trade because of ease and safety in travel and communication.

Rome ruled more of the known world for a longer period of time than any empire known to man. The Romans developed a high degree of skill in government. They gave wide freedom to local custom and religion, as was seen when Jesus and later Paul appeared before Roman judges. Pilate, it will be recalled, wanted to dismiss Roman jurisdiction over the case of Jesus and turn it back to the ecclesiastical courts because a matter of religion was at issue. Only when he was told that Jesus claimed kingship for himself and was stirring up political revolt did he accept jurisdiction and give judgment. Agrippa pointed out the same distinction when Paul appeared before him, and would have set Paul free had he not previously appealed to Rome. The Romans were firm in maintenance of public order and repression of revolt, but liberal in their attitude toward religion and local customs. The more peaceful a colonial administrator could keep the people, the more successful he was. Wars cost money. Rome was interested not in spending money, but in collecting money for the benefit of the Empire. Collection of revenue and maintenance of public order were therefore two of the most important problems facing the Roman administrator.

This struggle between local customs and public order confronted the Roman rulers continuously with difficult decisions of policy. Archelaus used too heavy a hand in enforcing public order and on complaint to Rome of an embassy from Judaea and Samaria he was removed from office in 6 A.D. Pilate yielded to mass protest in many minor matters of administration. However, he firmly refused to halt the building of an aqueduct for the water supply of Jerusalem with funds taken from the Temple treasury. When the protest went beyond what Pilate considered justifiable, he sent soldiers among the protesting group to silence the people by wounds and death.

This struggle between religion and Roman rule is shown in the New Testament record. Luke refers to "the Galileans whose blood Pilate had mingled with their sacrifices." Pilate, no doubt, believed these Galileans were using religion as a cloak for revolutionary activity. He may have had good grounds for his belief. In his address before the Council, Gamaliel refers to Judas, the Galilean, father of the Zealot movement and another revolutionary leader, Theudas. Barabbas, who was released at the time of Jesus' Crucifixion, was in prison for insurrection and murder. There was a vast amount of revolutionary activity, often violent, during New Testament days.

The Zealots found many followers among the people. Yet there were those who saw the weakness of their position. The priests and the more substantial people, like the Loyalists in colonial America, preferred to live in peace as a Roman colony. However, this attitude did not grow out of love for Rome such as the Loyalists had for Mother England; it derived from a realistic view of the situation. Any revolt against Rome was bound to end in failure; it was scarcely possible that Israel could destroy the Romans garrisoned in her land; and even if all of them were destroyed, the priests knew that Rome would not accept Israel's victory as her defeat. Armies sufficiently strong to crush any rebellion would be sent in. Little Israel against mighty Rome faced a contest so unequal that the foolhardy alone would undertake it.

Just the same, the priests did not like the 10 per cent tax on grain and the 20 per cent tax on wine and fruit, for such taxes were bound to decrease their income for religious purposes. They also knew it was possible through orderly channels to get things changed. Was not Archelaus removed as governor of Judaea and Samaria on protest from local leaders? Had they not got the Roman eagles, the bust of the Emperor, and the golden shields of Pilate removed from Jerusalem? True, they were not able to block the building of the aqueduct with Temple funds; yet they had continued to protest so vigorously that they did get the money repaid. The priests, knowing the folly of the sword, relied on public sentiment. The soundness of their judgment was borne out by the fact that they made the tithe and double-tithe taxes so unpopular and aroused so much resistance to their collection that they were discontinued and never again attempted.

The working motto of the orthodox religious leaders was "Love work, keep apart from politics, and have nothing to do with office." They called themselves "the Holy Nation," "the Kingdom of Priests," which for them meant that religion towered above all political considerations. Superior piety, knowledge of the law, and personal virtue made up their ideal. These qualities cannot be imparted or denied by the state, nor passed on by heredity. The priests might hesitate to say with Paul that "the powers that be are ordained of God," but their policy meant acceptance of "the powers that be" and making the best of a bad situation.

The attitude and action of the Zealots and the priests are a matter of record. It would be safe to assume that many other people who left no record wished for nothing more than the quiet of their homes and for this quiet paid, somewhat reluctantly, the price required. "We only live this life once," such men reasoned; "we must get what happiness we can while we can. There is no good destroying present felicity by struggling over conditions that cannot be changed."

The Zealots, however, despised reasonable men who sent embassies to Rome, and complacent men who sang to their children and paid their taxes. Romans were enemies of God; Romans had no right in the land. To pay tithe to the Romans was to betray God and country. Death was preferable to such betrayal.

Brushing aside reason and prudence, they appealed to long-repressed feelings and resentments. They spoke aloud what other men felt in their hearts. They blew upon smoldering coals and fanned them to blazing flames. Reaching into the past, they seized upon the dying words of Mattathias Maccabaeus, "My children, *be ye zealous* for the law, and give your lives for the covenant of your fathers. And call to remembrance the deeds of our fathers which they did in their generation: and receive great glory and an everlasting name." Hence their name Zealots.

The fact that Mattathias and two of his sons had died for their country added passion to the appeal. It was like Garibaldi's call for men willing to die for Italy and Churchill's promise of "blood, sweat, and tears." Every Jew knew of the exploits of the Maccabean family, for the death of the father and two of his sons had opened the way for one and a half centuries of liberty under the Maccabean line. The priests, realizing the revolutionary possibilities of the Maccabean story, excluded it from their teaching. Also there is no mention of the Maccabeans in the Talmud. Nevertheless, the story lived from mouth to mouth and enjoyed great popularity in a volume of four books.

Connecting himself in the popular mind with Mattathias Maccabaeus, Judas of Gamala won widespread attention. He coined the slogan "No God but Jehovah; no tax but to the temple; no friend but a Zealot." In 7 A.D. he gathered a large following, especially among the youth of the land, fell upon isolated garrisons of Roman soldiers, and took the lives of all he captured. He then turned his destructive power against collaborators with Rome. The country houses of the rich Sadducees and the barns of the wealthy friends of Rome were destroyed with fire. The daggers of his followers were quick to enter the rib of a Jew friendly to Rome as well as that of the Roman soldier or government agent. Terror gripped the land, for no one knew how or when the Zealots would strike or the extent of the damage that would be inflicted. For two months the hills of Galilee were covered with smoke. Every day brought stories of more bloodshed. As a boy Jesus quite possibly saw the fires from the hillside of Nazareth and watched the people as they huddled together for mutual protection.

Roman soldiers were dispatched at once to put down the rebellion, and within two months the strong arm of Rome had crushed all open opposition and put Judas of Gamala to death. His four sons, Jacobus, Simon, Menahem, and Eleazar, continued guerrilla warfare until each of them fell in battle or took his own life to prevent capture by the Romans. A grandson of Judas fighting with the last defenders of Judean freedom on the rocks of Nasada boasted that as his family were the first to take up arms against the Romans, so they would be the last to lay them down. By his order and with their own consent, nine hundred of his soldiers shut themselves up in their fortress and destroyed themselves by fire so the Romans would have only ashes for their victory.

The Zealot movement continued to be active during the lifetime of Jesus. It was an underground movement of undetermined size feared alike by the Romans and by the Jews who co-operated with the Romans.

Josephus in his account of the fall of Jerusalem (70 A.D.) pictures the Zealots as one of three major parties defending the city. He says that even while Roman soldiers surrounded Jerusalem these factions were "at war with each other. The citizens were their common prize, and those of the people who discountenanced their iniquity became the prey of both. . . . They [the people of Jerusalem] suffered nothing worse at the hands of the Romans than what they inflicted upon each other." Allowing for the obvious pro-Roman bias of Josephus, truth enough remains to reveal the tragedy of a rigid patriotism that loved only those of its own nation who thought, felt, and acted like themselves. The Zealots leave a tragic picture. Their zeal consumed friend more effectively than foe; their fires left Jewish homes in ashes but Rome unhurt by the flame. Their irrational revolt brought death and destruction to those they would make free. Their love of country destroyed the country they loved.

Jesus saw clearly the problem of conflict between Israel and Rome. The priests tried to get him on the horns of a dilemma by forcing him to come out for or against paying the Roman tax, but he avoided taking the side of either priest or Zealot, pointing out that man has an obligation both to government and to religion.

Jesus knew the tragedy that strife with Rome held for his people and lamented, "O Jerusalem, Jerusalem! . . . How often would I have gathered your children together as a hen gathers her brood under her wings, and you would not! Behold, your house is forsaken . . ." "Would that even today you knew the things that make for peace! But now they are hid from your eyes. For the days shall come upon you, when your enemies will cast up a bank about you and surround you, and hem you in on every side, and dash you to the ground, you and your children within you, and they will not leave one stone upon another in you; because you did not know the time of your visitation."

Nevertheless, Jesus chose a Zealot by the name of Simon as

one of his apostles. He also chose Matthew, the tax collector, collaborator and tool of Roman domination. In terms of Jesus' attitude toward Jewish national aspirations, the choice of the one canceled out the choice of the other. He reached above national pride to a universal concern.

Long years have passed since Zealots contended with priests and Jews fought against Romans, yet the principles that dominated them continue to operate in the modern world. The record of history is re-enacted in the events reported in the daily newspaper. Time relationships tend to disappear when we realize that history is but yesterday's newspaper and men today simply the sons of the past. Love of nation and desire for freedom arouse men as deeply now as ever. Zealot, priest, and Roman clash; blood is spilled; cities destroyed. So loud is the voice of conflict that few hear the voice that said, "O Jerusalem, Jerusalem! . . . How often would I have gathered your children together as a hen gathers her brood under her wings, and you would not. Behold, your house is forsaken!"

The things that make for peace are hidden from our eyes quite as effectively as they were from the eyes of those who heard the words of Jesus and his apostles. Jet airplanes, atomic bombs, germs, armies and navies—in these we put our trust. Suspicion divides us from our brothers and we hide in fear from one another behind man-made curtains. Death and destruction reverse their natural role and pose as bearers of confidence and peace.

Is it fair to ask, "If Jesus were here today where would he stand?" A Zealot brandishing modern weapons in the cause of freedom? A priest adopting every expedient to win national advantage? A Roman committed to the perpetuation of the *status quo?* Would he be a Democrat, a Republican, a union member, a chamber of commerce director, an America, a Russian, a white man, a yellow man, or a black man? How ridiculous it is to suggest that the Lord of Life can be identified with any group. Yet how easily we fall into the error of making Jesus one with whatever group claims our allegiance. It is easier to make Jesus into our own image than to remake ourselves after his likeness. Simon, the Zealot, was wiser than many Christians today. He did not try to change Jesus into a Zealot. Rather he changed himself into a humble apostle of the Lord.

The mention of the name of Simon Zealot among the apostles who awaited the coming of the Holy Spirit shows his continuing loyalty to the Lord and his identification with the early Christian Church. Aside from his membership in the Zealot group and his loyalty as an apostle there is, unfortunately, no information about him. Whether he came to Jesus with blood on his hands or smoke in his cloak we do not know. How deep was his commitment to the Zealot movement or how much his political attitudes changed under the influence of Jesus is not recorded. What he thought about the tax collector, Matthew, can only be guessed, but both men held a common love of Jesus Christ.

In the lists of the apostles given by Matthew and Luke the name of Simon, the Zealot, is coupled with that of Judas Iscariot. Does this point to a common attitude on the question of political freedom and the means of attaining it, as some think? Was there common ground between them or was their position in the lists of the apostles merely accidental?

What happened to Simon Zealot after the death of Jesus? Did he, as tradition suggests, take the Gospel to Persia, Suamii Weriosphora, Jerusalem, or "that Island in the Sea" (Britain)? To the fish on a book that forms the symbol for the shield of Simon Zealot is sometimes added a battle-ax or a saw. Does this indicate the manner of his death?

There are many questions to be asked about Simon Zealot. Unfortunately there are no sure answers for any of them. Beyond knowledge of his name we must rely on imagination until the great day when we shall know as we are known.

12
Judas, Son of James

SAINT JUDE'S DAY October 28

The Collect

O Almighty God, who hast built thy Church upon the foundation of the Apostles and Prophets, Jesus Christ himself being the head corner-stone; Grant us so to be joined together in unity of spirit by their doctrine, that we may be made an holy temple acceptable unto thee; through the same Jesus Christ our Lord. *Amen.*

WITH THE SHEPHERDS WHO KEPT WATCH OVER their flocks in Bethlehem at the time of Jesus' birth was a little boy called Jude. He was too young to care for the sheep but he made himself useful running errands and doing any tasks that lay within his ability. When the glory of the Lord shone round about the shepherds and the birth of the Christ was announced, the boy Jude went with the shepherds to see the newborn Child. After the others had returned to their sheep the lad lingered entranced with the beauty of the babe. The mother, seeing the wonder in his eyes, placed the Child in his arms. Trembling with happiness, he held the baby Jesus for a few moments of unforgettable joy. Years passed; the lad grew to manhood and was called by Jesus to be one of his chosen apostles. Thus, according to legend, there was a close tie between Jude and Jesus. However, Scripture merely refers to him as Judas, son of James.

The years of Judas' childhood, his early interest in Jesus, his call to apostleship, and his reaction to the Gospel ministry of our Lord are all unrecorded. There is vagueness even in the record of his name, for he is called by Matthew, Lebbaeus; by Mark, Thaddaeus; and by Luke, Judas, son of James. In Aramaic *Lebbaeus* means courageous or hearty while *Thaddaeus* means lively, vivacious. These designations may be taken to indicate the character of the apostle, but it is unlikely they were intended to convey that meaning.

Judas, son of James, spoke once and only once in the recorded words of the New Testament. At the end of Jesus' last night with his disciples Judas asked a question that gave Jesus an opportunity to restate important aspects of his teaching. Since this is the only record given of him, it may be well to return in imagination to this sacred occasion and to try to recapture the experience as Judas lived it.

Death was an uninvited guest in the upper room where Jesus met with his chosen Twelve. Judas, son of James, sat with the Twelve, seeing only what they saw: the table, the simple food, Jesus, and the apostles. For the apostles this Passover Feast did not differ from those observed since childhood at home or, more recently, in fellowship with the Master. True, the Scribes and Pharisees were bitter in opposition and whispers had been heard that the life of Jesus was in jeopardy. However, this was not entirely new, for danger had been a companion since the early days of apostleship. The present danger would pass as had others before it.

Before the disciples had been seated at the table Jesus had taken occasion to teach them a lesson in humility. Unconscious of the meaning of the occasion, the disciples upon entering the upper room had jostled and contended one with another for the honor of sitting next to Jesus. Little had they realized that tonight death occupied the seat of honor. Jesus alone knew that he "had come from God and was going to God." In full consciousness of his identity with God, our Lord had taken a towel and gone from one to the other washing their feet. Blind as they were to the realities of the situation, they had sensed the presence of God in this lowly act of service. Humbled, they had taken their places at the table of the Lord.

Seated now at the table were Jesus, his disciples, and the unseen guest. The towel had been laid aside in anticipation of the well-known ritual of the Passover Feast. Jesus surprised the apostles by instituting a new observance. Taking the bread from the table, he gave it to Judas, son of James, and to the others, saying, "This is my body which is broken for you"; and likewise he gave them the cup, "This cup is the new covenant in my blood." It was a solemn moment. In the past many times had they shared the fellowship of the table; together they had observed the Passover Feast. Yet in some strange way this was different. Bread—body: wine—blood. What was the meaning of it all? "Do this, as often as you drink it, in remembrance of me," he added. It is doubtful if any who took the bread and wine grasped the meaning of the event. Yet no one asked to have it interpreted, for all realized that this was a moment when the present remakes the past for the larger purpose of the future, and God is mediated to his children.

With this holy background Jesus poured out his heart to Judas and the others. He likened their lives as bound to him in God as a vine is joined to the branches, warned them of the persecution that awaited them, and offered up the high priestly prayer beginning "Father, the hour has come; glorify thy Son that the Son may glorify thee." As the evening drew to an end his heart filled with tenderness and he tried to comfort his disciples. "Let not your hearts be troubled;" he said, "believe in God, believe also in me." Realizing that tomorrow he must bear the Cross, he promised, "I will not leave you desolate; I will come to you.

Yet a little while, and the world will see me no more, but you will see me." Judas, son of James, not knowing about the Cross or the fellowship of the resurrected Christ, asked, "Lord, how is it that you will manifest yourself to us, and not to the world?" Jesus replied, "If a man loves me, he will keep my word, and my Father will love him, and we will come to him and make our home with him. . . . Peace I leave with you; my peace I give to you. . . . If you loved me, you would have rejoiced, because I go to the Father. . . . I will no longer talk much with you, for the ruler of this world is coming. He has no power over me. . . . Rise, let us go hence."

Many scholars believe that the chapter in John's Gospel which contains this question of Judas and the reply of the Master should be placed after Chapters 15, 16, and 17. With this arrangement, the question by Judas and the answer from Jesus are the last words spoken before Gethsemane and Calvary. The importance of the exchange is thus heightened for them and for Christians of all time.

"Lord, how is it you will manifest yourself to us, and not to the world?" Judas, son of James, as he asked this question, knew that during Jesus' earthly ministry everyone with physical vision had been able to look upon Him. He did not know that after the Resurrection Jesus would be seen not by "the world" but only through the eyes of faith. The guards at the tomb did not see the risen Lord, but he was seen by Mary Magdalene, Peter, John, the Twelve, and upward of five hundred believers at one time. How was this possible? Jesus answered, "If a man loves me, he will keep my word, and my Father will love him, and we will come to him and make our home with him." Jesus was saying, "The secret, Judas, lies in a man's heart. The man of love is the man who sees."

One day, sitting around a campfire in the mountains of Western Maryland, a group of young people listened to a young woman describe the birds of the area. She told the names of birds she had seen in the few days she had been in camp, described what they looked like, and gave their calls. She paused several times to point out and to identify the birds whose songs came across the evening sky. The camp was familiar ground to most of these youth. Year after year they had returned to enjoy the forest, the lake, the playgrounds, and the cottages. But the beautiful birds who made the woods their home had not existed to any except the bird lover. The beauty of nature is seen by the heart of love and by no other.

Haydon, the historical painter, visited Edinburgh in 1820 and dined with Sir Walter Scott, Jeffrey, and other celebrities. He wrote his impression of the occasion as follows:

> Jeffrey had a singular expression—poignant, bitter, piercing—as if his countenance never lighted up but at the perception of some weakness in human nature. Whatever you praise to Jeffrey, he directly clutches at some error that you did not perceive. Whatever your praise to Scott, he heartily joins with yourself, and directs your attention to some additional beauty. The face of Scott is the expression of a man whose great pleasure it has been to shake nature by the hand; which to point at her with his finger has certainly, from his expression, been the chief joy of Jeffrey.

The open hand or the pointed finger. What a difference they make in what the eye sees. If one loves he sees beauty in the natural world, goodness in his fellows, and potential for the best on every hand.

Beyond vision, love gives obedience. In answer to Judas' question, Jesus said, "If any man loves me, he will keep my word." The man of love does not need one thousand and one rules of "do and don't," for love fulfills all the law and the commandments. In Jesus' day the attempt to govern all the minute details of life by rules and regulations had gone so far that only experts could hope to know right from wrong. The common man was thus shut out from God by the very means that were intended to draw him to the Father. When confronted with this situation Jesus went to the heart of the matter, declaring that there were two great commandments: "You shall love the Lord your God with all your heart, and with all your soul, and with all your mind"; and "You shall love your neighbor as yourself." Those who love need no other commandments, for the rightness of their central attitudes makes right all action.

When Paul wrote to the church at Corinth he spoke freely of the many weaknesses that beset her people. The church was divided into four warring factions claiming as their spiritual leaders Paul, Apollos, Cephas, and Christ. Ugly as church quarrels are, there was an even worse situation, for they were tolerating in their fellowship immorality of a type that even pagans condemned—a member of the church was living with his father's wife. Added to this scandal was the sight of Christian brother going to law against Christian brother to settle personal differences. Even the house of God was not kept sacred; for, gathering to eat the Lord's Supper, some were left without adequate food while others ate too much and a few were actually drunk. How did Paul meet this distressing situation? Did Paul in anger disown this wayward church? Did he point the finger of shame? Quite the opposite. In the spirit of his Master, Paul poured out his heart in a beautiful hymn of love. "Make love your aim," he urges, "earnestly desire the spiritual gifts," for of all the abiding gifts of God "the greatest . . . is love."

"If a man loves me," continued Jesus in his answer to Judas, son of James, "my Father will love him." Man's love for God meets the responsive love of God for man. It is true, of course, that God loves all men all the time. The love of God, like the sun, constantly floods the earth and is the source of all life. Man can shut out the light of the sun by withdrawing into his house, closing the shutters, or drawing the blinds; but the man who dwells in self-made darkness does not thereby destroy the sun. The sun forever shines and enters into every house the instant the blinds are opened and the shutters thrown wide. Even so the love of God surrounds every man. When man throws open the window of his heart the love comes flooding upon him. "If a man loves me—my Father will love him." The Risen Lord reaffirmed the promise when he said, "Lo, I am with you always." The responding love of God awaits the open heart of love.

The fruit of this loving fellowship with God, Judas was told by Jesus, is peace, joy, and confidence. "Peace I leave with you," he said, "my peace I give to you." The peace of Jesus is not a release from burdens and conflicts but an inner resource of strength that keeps a place of quiet at the very center of the hurricane of life. A short time before Judas' question, Jesus had reminded the apostles, "In the world you have tribulation." "But," he added, "be of good cheer, I have overcome the world." The Christian is not entirely delivered from any of the normal tribulations of life. Sickness, suffering, conflict, labor, sacrifice, separation, death—all may have a part in the day-by-day life of the Christian. Yet with love in his heart the Christian has the golden key to peace. Whatever happens the man of love knows that it will work together for good because back of the event is the care of a loving God. God is not going to answer the cry for bread with a stone or the request for fish with a serpent. If earthly parents know how to give good gifts, how much more will the heavenly Father care for his children.

As our Lord continued to speak to Judas and to the other disciples he said, "If you loved me, you would have rejoiced, because I go to the Father." Of all times when rejoicing seemed out of the question, it was this hour when Jesus was going to the Father. By the promise of rejoicing at the time of death's separation Jesus does not deny the experience of grief. Mary Magdalene wept at the tomb of Jesus and, rather than a rebuke, the Master gave her a tender and understanding revelation of himself. Our Lord himself wept beside the tomb of Lazarus and so great was his grief that the neighbors standing beside him commented, "See how he loved him."

Our generation is restrained in the public expression of grief. This social custom may or may not be the best for people whose loved ones are returning to God. The feeling of grief and the expression of sorrow are in no wise unbecoming to a Christian. If Mary was unrebuked for her tears and if Jesus wept in his sadness we, too, may weep when our hearts, like theirs, are heavy with grief. The joy that Jesus promised the Christian is the knowledge that beyond the tears of separation is the joy of reunion. Beyond Lazarus' grave is the restored fellowship given by Him who raised him from the dead. After the tears of Mary Magdalene is the gladness of hearing Jesus' voice, "Mary," and the ecstasy of clasping his feet, "Rabboni!" The joy promised by our Lord meets the hurt of the human heart at its deepest need. The love of God is the only balm for the left-lonely heart. This balm alone can heal man's sorrowing soul and bring rejoicing in his darkest hour.

Concluding his reply to Judas, Jesus said, "I will no longer talk much with you, for the ruler of this world is coming. He has no power over me." Before another sunset the man who was speaking these words would have great nails driven into his hands and feet and would be suspended between heaven and earth until life slowly ebbed away. What does he mean when he says, "the ruler of this world is coming. He has no power over me"? It seemed that the ruler of this world had plenty of power and did not hesitate to use it to destroy the life of the Master.

In this concluding word of confidence Jesus is looking beyond Pilate to the Father in heaven, beyond the Cross to the open tomb, beyond the events of the coming day to the verdict of eternity. During the long hours in Gethsemane the flesh would do battle with the spirit and cry out in agony, "My Father, if it be possible, let this cup pass from me." On the Cross a dark cloud would pass over him and he would cry, "My God, my God, why hast thou forsaken me?" Aside from these inward struggles our Lord would maintain the poise and confidence expressed to Judas and to the other disciples. On trial before Pilate he declared, "You would have no power over me unless it had been given you from above." Among his last words was the simple statement, "Father, into thy hands I commit my spirit," which befits the prayer of a little child lying down to confident restful sleep more than the agonizing prayer of a man whose soul is about to depart from his body.

The confidence Jesus displayed in his closing hours grows out of a life ruled by love; a life whose values are set not in time but in eternity, where God is more real than Caesar; a life whose treasures are laid up in heaven rather than on the earth.

Paul Geren, writing the autobiographical story of Peter Strong, relates an experience during the Burma campaign that illustrates confidence growing out of love:

One night at dusk, three soldier friends and he stood up on a high bank and sang a song, because it was the end of day and it was rather quiet. The song was "When I Survey the Wondrous Cross." When they had finished, "My richest gain I count but loss, and pour contempt on all my pride," and were about to go on to the second stanza, Peter talked to himself in one of those conversations which are finished long before they can be told, even in the taking of a breath between the stanzas of a hymn:

"What if in the singing of this song a shell comes over and gets you?"

Peter answered himself, "It would be all right, it would be everlastingly all right. Now nothing can be lost, nothing can be forgotten. Nothing can begin, nothing can end. We have struggled, and nothing can unhand us. We have learned, and nothing can rob us. We have begotten, and nothing can deny us. We have seen, and nothing can blind us. We have loved, and nothing can destroy us. If now, when we have our gay heads lifted to the clear sky, when we are glorying with this joyful noise, if now it comes, it is all right, it is everlastingly all right."

When they were on the third verse, a shell did come. When it whistled, the quartette hit the dirt as one man, leaving the song awkwardly suspended at "sorrow and love." Peter's heart was beating fast, his breathing was heavy. He was as fully delivered over to the adrenalin as ever. . . .

When the adrenalin had ebbed somewhat and he could realize the shell had not hit him, Peter grasped the congruity: "Sorrow and love flow mingled down!" Christ is on the Cross. Sorrow and love. The mother is bearing the child. Sorrow and love. The dying soldier lies in his comrade's arms. Sorrow and love.

The shell had flown just a bit over Peter's crouched body and hit a man somewhat behind him. Only one shell that time—and only one man. But had it come to him that time, when he was with "sorrow and love," he vowed it would have been all right, everlastingly all right.

For an instant when the shell whistled Peter had hit the dirt with fear pounding his heart, but before and after the shell came he felt that death for him "would have been all right, everlastingly all right." In this confidence saints of all ages have faced the supreme sacrifice and have found victory.

Those who live ruled by love cannot be robbed of their property, for their treasure is in heaven; they cannot be isolated in jail, for as Hudson Taylor said, "You may hedge me about but you can't roof me over"; they cannot be controlled by threat and fear, for they know only one fear, the displeasure of God; nor can they be destroyed, for if their bodies perish their spirits only thereby increase in power and effectiveness. It is doubtful that Judas at the time understood all the wonderful truths spoken by Jesus in response to his question. As the Risen Lord revealed himself to the Twelve, it became more clear what Jesus meant by "manifesting himself." The world is still ignorant of the manifest glory of the Living Lord. Today, as always, only those who love him see his glory revealed. This is the mystery and grandeur of the Christian experience.

Judas, son of James, is identified by the Roman Catholic Church as Judas, brother of James, who was the brother (cousin, as they interpret it) of our Lord. We have already seen that the Roman Catholics consider the apostle James, son of Alphaeus, the same person as James, the brother of our Lord. It is true that the King James Version refers to Judas as "brother of James," but the Revised and Revised Standard Versions, along with the commentaries on the subject, agree that the proper translation should be "son of James."

Based on the identification of Judas as brother of James, Catholic scholarship considers Judas, the apostle, to be the author of the Epistle of Jude. In this case, Jude's calling himself "servant of Jesus Christ" is attributed to modesty and the desire not to boast of blood relationship to Jesus. But evidence against this identification is the seventeenth verse of Jude, which says, "You must remember, beloved, the predictions of the apostles of our Lord Jesus Christ; they said to you . . ." This verse, Protestant scholars agree, plainly indicates that the author of the Epistle of Jude was not an apostle of Jesus Christ.

The name of Judas in the list of those at Pentecost shows that he remained faithful after the Crucifixion. Jesus' gratitude that none of those chosen (save the son of perdition) was lost makes it reasonable to assume that Judas endured the privations and sufferings common in the early Christian Church.

An ancient tradition recorded by Eusebius in his *Ecclesiastical History* identifies Thaddaeus with the healing of Abgar, King of Edessa, who was stricken with leprosy. When Abgar learned through contact with Sabinus, the Roman proconsul of Syria, of the healing miracles performed by Jesus of Nazareth, he wrote to him the following letter:

Abgar Arschama, Prince of the Country, to Jesus, Saviour and Benefactor, who hast appeared in the province of Jerusalem. Greeting:

I have heard tell of thee and of the cures which thou workest, without using remedies of herbs. For from what one hears, thou makest the blind to see and the lame to walk; thou dost cleanse the lepers and cast out unclean spirits; thou dost cure those afflicted with chronic ills, and even thou dost raise the dead. When I heard all this of thee, I said to myself, it must mean one of two things; either thou art a God descended from heaven to work these miracles, or else thou art the Son of God, thou who achievest such wonders. This is the occasion of my writing. I implore thee to take the trouble to visit me, and to cure me of the disease from which I suffer. I have also heard that the Jews murmur against thee and wish thee harm. Now I possess a city, small but beautiful, and that will be sufficient for us both.

The courier presented this letter to Philip and Andrew, who took the message to Jesus. The letter was answered by Thomas in Jesus' behalf as follows:

Happy is he who believeth on me without having seen me for it is written of me, "He that seeth me will not believe on me, and he that seeth me not, will believe and live." As to the matter of which thou hast written, asking me to come unto thee, I must first fulfil here all those things for which I have been sent. When these are fulfilled I ascend unto him that hath sent me, and when I have ascended I will send one of my disciples, who shall cure thee of thy ills, and will give life to thee and to those that are with thee. May thy city be blessed, and may no enemy ever bear rule over her.

Later tradition, given by Moses of Chorene, 460 A.D., records that after Jesus ascended to heaven Thomas sent Thaddaeus to Edessa. Arriving at Edessa, Thaddaeus' face radiated such glory that he was recognized at once as the envoy of the Great Healer. With a touch Thaddaeus healed Abgar of leprosy and as a token that the miracle was performed by the power of Jesus Christ gave to Abgar a portrait of the Master drawn during his lifetime. This legend accounts for the fact that Jude is sometimes pictured as wearing an image of the Saviour about his neck or carrying an image of Him in his hand.

After many other sick persons had been healed by Thaddaeus, the story continued, King Abgar and his entire court were converted and baptized. From that time the name of Thaddaeus has been honored in all Edessa.

This ancient legend leaves in doubt whether Thaddaeus is one of the Twelve and thus to be identified with Labbaeus and Judas, son of James, or one of the seventy called by our Lord. Like so much legendary material, it is beautiful but will not stand strict historical investigation.

In spite of doubtful historicity the Armenians continue to honor Thaddaeus and Bartholomew as their fathers in Christ. Not content with two of the Twelve as their founders, the Armenians also claim that Simon Zealot, Andrew, and the thirteenth apostle, Matthias, preached the Gospel in their land. Dr. Edgar J. Goodspeed reports that the Armenian Church, under the influence of Louise Nalbandian, an Armenian scholar at Stanford University, is at this time translating the Bible into its modern spoken language. This bringing of the Gospel into the speech of the people is being undertaken with all devotion to the apostles whom they honor as their spiritual forebears.

The fact that Judas, son of James, bore the same name as the betrayer, Judas Iscariot, caused him loss of esteem among the early Christians. As a result, it is said, his name was never invoked except when all other saints had been appealed to in vain. Judas, son of James, has thus become the patron saint of the desperate and the despairing. Since he is so seldom invoked except in the most desperate cases, he has more time and energy for those who call upon him than do the popular saints. He is said never to fail the few who call upon his name.

In addition to the stories of his labor in Edessa there is tradition that Judas preached in Persia and Armenia and died in agonizing torture from the wounds of arrows. The apostle who questioned Jesus in the upper room when death was an unseen guest thus goes at last to the Upper Room where there is no death. He learns anew the manifest glory of God. There is no question asked, for face to face he sees the Lord.

13
Judas Iscariot

WITH CLANG OF ARMOR AND GLARE OF TORCH THE soldiers marched through the darkness into the Garden of Gethsemane. The clamor aroused the disciples from their sleep and our Lord from the agony of his prayer. Quickly the band of soldiers surrounded Jesus and his little group of disciples. From among the soldiers Judas Iscariot stepped forth, saying, "Hail, Master," and kissed him. Jesus rebuked him, saying, "Judas, would you betray the Son of man with a kiss?"

Even as he kissed his Master, Judas strapped about his waist thirty pieces of silver, the price paid by the High Priests for his treachery. The thirty pieces of silver, John's Gospel tells us, found company with other coins previously stolen from the common purse of the apostles.

The shock of finding such wickedness among the Twelve chosen to be apostles of Jesus Christ has not diminished through the years. Jesus recoiled from it, saying, "Did I not choose you, the twelve, and one of you is a devil?" To betray innocent blood, to sell a friend for silver, and to do it under the mask of a friendly kiss surely is the work of the devil. No name in history is weighted with such shame as the name of Judas Iscariot.

In spite of this fact—or it might be more accurate to say because of this fact—Judas is a character of intense interest to people everywhere. More than any other apostle he has commanded the attention of poets, dramatists, and writers of fiction. The morality plays, the folk stories, and the folk customs of the people make Judas a central character. Today in the smallest rural chapel or in the largest city church the announcement of a sermon on Judas brings a quickening of interest. This interest grows out of our fascination with wrongdoing. Crime and evil occupy a large percentage of space in newspapers, magazines, books, movies, and television programs. The most religious people avidly read the details of murders, divorces, thievery, and other scandalous conduct. The more wicked the person, the more sure is the interest in his actions.

Judas is a very dramatic figure. The symbols that cluster about him stir the imagination—the bag, the thirty pieces of silver, the kiss, the tree, the rope. These symbols have passed into common speech. John's account of Judas' departure from the upper room to fulfill his treacherous betrayal ends with these words, "He went out and it was night." The contrast between Jesus and Judas, between the fellowship of the broken bread and the conspiracy of the traitor, between the Light of the World and the darkness in Judas' heart—all this is gathered in the simple words, "He went out and it was night." Rembrandt in his greatest masterpiece never made better use of light and shadow.

Shakespeare knew the appeal of the villain. Shylock is as famous as Portia, Iago as Othello, Brutus as Julius Caesar, Lady Macbeth as Banquo. Yet when all the villains of history and of literature are placed beside Judas, they seem inferior to him. Judas was not the first or the last person to betray a friend. Why does his betrayal put him in a class by himself? In part, because of the scriptural record, which gives no hint of favorable characteristics or extenuating circumstances that might explain or mitigate his crime. But, more, Judas was so evil because Jesus was so good. The crime was of such enormous proportions because it was directed against Him who alone among men is without fault. The brighter the light, the deeper the shadow. Judas stood in the presence of the Light of Lights, even the Son of God; therefore his darkness was midnight and his betrayal the greatest of sins.

Prior to the time of our Lord, Judas was an honored name in Israel. One Judas Maccabaeus in 167 B.C. had led the successful revolt against Greece that won independence for his people. In the list of Jesus' ancestors the name Judas is mentioned by Luke. Jesus had a brother by the name of Judas. Another Judas, son of James, was one of the apostles. Gamaliel mentions a Judas of Galilee who led an unsuccessful revolt against Rome in the time of Cyrenius. Paul stayed with a Judas in Damascus and had Judas Barsabas as a traveling companion on the journey to Antioch. But the evil deed of Judas Iscariot left such a deep impression on the human mind that since his time the name has disappeared from common usage. Today no one would call a son Judas.

Considering that Jesus had a large number of disciples from whom to select the Twelve, we are faced with two questions. First, why did a man like Judas choose to be one of the apostles? Second, why did Jesus choose Judas to be in his inner group?

The fact that Judas voluntarily placed himself among Jesus' disciples makes it reasonable to assume that there was a side to his nature that the tragic events at the end of his life did not reveal. That Judas before he became an apostle had a yearning for the good life and that he followed Jesus to find fulfillment of this yearning is the most natural and obvious deduction. There was no pressure to join this select group of followers. Indeed, Jesus discouraged many who seemed very likely prospects. There is no reason to assume that, when chosen by Jesus, Judas was any other than a sincere and honest apostle.

Was Jesus deceived in Judas? Jesus was a remarkable judge of human personality. He read Nathanael's character and Peter's nature on first sight. He understood the woman at the well of Samaria before she said a word. Did he fail to see the inherent weakness in Judas?

John says, "Jesus knew from the first . . . who it was that should betray him." This seems to indicate that with foreknowledge Judas was chosen for the evil deed he performed. In rejecting this idea, Dr. A. B. Bruce comments, "It is not credible that Iscariot was chosen merely to be a traitor, as an actor might be chosen by a theatre manager to play the part of Iago. The end pointed at in the Scripture quoted might be ultimately served by his being chosen, but that end was not the motive of the choice. We may regard these two points as certain: on the one hand, that Judas did not become a follower of Jesus with treacherous intention; and on the other, that Jesus did not elect Judas to be one of the Twelve because he fore-knew that he would eventually become a traitor." The evil action of Judas, like all human evil, was not foreordained but came as a result of wrong choices.

The long discussions by theologically minded writers on the dilemma of the foreknowledge of Jesus versus the moral freedom of Judas throw no light on this tragic apostle. God foreknows all things, yet gives man freedom of choice. Foreknowledge versus freedom is no more the problem of Judas and Jesus than it is the problem of God and mankind. When called as an apostle Judas had possibilities of becoming a great Christian leader; he developed in the opposite direction. Why should a modern sinner find this difficult to understand? Is this not the tragic history of Everyman?

John states that Judas "was a thief, and as he had the money box he used to take what was put into it." The writers of the first three Gospels fail to mention this fact. The words of John stand as one of the oldest records portraying the character of Judas and on this record Judas was a thief before he was a traitor. It would seem from the nature of this misdoing that it was a secret sin unknown at the time to the Twelve and also unknown to Jesus, at least in its early stages.

It was the custom of James Smithson to illustrate the wide margins of his Bible. Opposite the story of Judas betraying his Master he drew a picture of a baby lying on a cradle pillow with a sweet face and large wondering eyes. Beneath the picture he wrote "Judas Iscariot." One can believe that on his cradle pillow Judas was a sweet innocent baby and that when he joined the Twelve, he was "called to be a saint." That he turned traitor is one of the tragedies of the New Testament and of human history, a tragedy deepened by realization that the traitor was potentially a man of God.

What prompted Judas to betrayal? The money bag may be the answer. The author of Timothy warned that "the love of money is the root of all evils." At the heart of most social problems is an economic base. Prostitution, gambling, and alcoholic beverages are the unholy trinity that account for a large majority of the problems of the police and the courts. They exist as great social problems not alone because of the weakness and sins of individual men and women but because they are organized into very profitable businesses. If profit seeking could be eliminated, the way would be open for effective steps to eradicate or to control them.

The prophet Amos speaks of selling "the righteous for silver, and the needy for a pair of shoes." Ezekiel warns of "polluting God" for handfuls of barley and for pieces of bread. Surely these prophets would condemn our poor housing which creates slums and wickedness. From these conditions a few people profit handsomely while the community at large pays and the slum dwellers degenerate.

The full truth of the temptation of money is not with the cynics who suggest that every man has his price, nor with the scholars who say all history is an extension of economic interests; but surely desire for money is a powerful motivation for evil. There is an old rhyme that points a moral all may ponder:

Still as of old
Man by himself is priced,
For thirty pieces Judas sold
Himself, not Christ.

If the author of Timothy was not 100 per cent right in assigning "love of money" as the root of all evil, he nevertheless had a sizable amount of truth in his observation.

The Scripture story gives strong support to love of money as motivation for Judas' betrayal. Great scholars of the early Church, Chrysostom, Origen, and Thomas Aquinas, accepted this position. John Ruskin considered Judas "a common money-lover." Dr. J. D. Jones, a more recent writer, agrees. "In the plain words of the Scripture," he maintains, "what prompted him to this crime was greed! 'He was a thief,' says John, 'and pilfered from the common purse.' Greed had already made him a thief —in the end it made him a traitor."

However, most modern writers on Judas consider greed inadequate motivation to explain the known facts about Judas. The amount of money involved in the betrayal—thirty pieces of silver—is estimated to be fifteen or twenty dollars. Allowing for difference in money value, it was still a very small sum. Some have used the smallness of the bribe to indicate the scorn of the rulers for Jesus. Others have imagined Judas bargaining with the rulers for more money and yielding to the paltry sum only when it became obvious it was the most he could obtain. However the imagination fills in these missing gaps, the scriptural fact remains that the amount given was thirty pieces of silver: a sum that would never tempt a loyal man to betray one he loved unless there was some disaffection preceding or accompanying the evil act.

If Judas betrayed his Lord for money, why did he hang himself when he saw the consequences of his betrayal? A man so greedy for money that he stole petty cash from the common purse, and sold his Master for thirty pieces of silver, must have had some side to his character that these facts do not reveal.

Why the sudden remorse? Why did he wait to see the results of his crime? Why was he disturbed at the consequences of his betrayal? The coins in his purse should have been comfort enough for a man who was simply a thief and a traitor.

Searching the Scripture for further motivation, some have suggested vindictiveness. Judas may have betrayed Jesus to get revenge for the rebuke given when Mary anointed the feet of the Master with costly ointment. Judas complained about this act of devotion as waste, asking, "Why was this ointment not sold for three hundred denarii and given to the poor?" Jesus, however, commended the act of love. "Let her alone," said Jesus, "let her keep it for the day of my burial. The poor you always have with you, but you do not always have me." This mild rebuke was almost identical with the correction given the disciples for an identical fault recorded in Matthew and in Mark. It revealed no bitterness either on the part of Jesus or of Judas. It did not compare with the reprimand given Peter when Jesus said to him, "Get behind me, Satan! You are a hindrance to me; for you are not on the side of God, but of men." It is difficult to see how these words to Judas could be so resented as to cause him to betray Jesus.

Since it is hard to sustain vindictiveness by the incident of the anointing alone, reference is made to the time Jesus said, "Did I not choose you, the twelve, and one of you is a devil?" In recording the incident the writer, desiring to make the meaning clear to the reader, added, "He spoke of Judas the son of Simon Iscariot, for he, one of the twelve, was to betray him." But those who heard Jesus say, "One of you is a devil," had no idea of whom he spoke. To them it was a dark saying. This word of Jesus, concealed as it was from the other eleven, could not have greatly influenced Judas' attitude.

Instead of pointing out Judas publicly as a traitor, Jesus carefully concealed that fact from others. To the last moment he sought to win Judas by especial love and affection. To be given the first sop, bread dipped in wine, was the highest honor at a feast. Jesus, instead of holding Judas up to scorn before the other disciples, actually did quite the opposite—he gave the sop to Judas.

Leslie Weatherhead says that, among the ruins of the first century, archaeologists have found many common cups with mottoes on them. One of the popular mottoes uses the very words, "Do what you have come to do." In our modern slang it would be "Do it now." Weatherhead speculates that when Jesus gave Judas his last word, "What you are going to do, do quickly," he was quoting the motto on the cup used for the wine, symbol of his blood. In this way he made a last desperate effort to reach the heart of Judas by an appeal to the fellowship of the cup in the hope of saving him from his treachery. This speculation may lack factual accuracy, but it is unquestionably accurate in presenting the character of Jesus. No, Judas could find nothing in the words or actions of Jesus to arouse a vindictive spirit.

An important factor in a study of Judas is that he was the only apostle from Judea. He came from Kerioth, as his name Iscariot indicates. The Judeans spoke a different dialect from the Galileans. Even the serving girl in the Temple knew that Peter was a Galilean when he spoke as he warmed himself by the fire. The Galileans, being farther from the Temple, were never very strict in their observation of the rules of ceremonial purity. Much of the controversy over washed hands, the tithe of mint and cumin, observation of Sabbath regulations, and the like represents conflicts between Galilee and Judea. Thus Judas, the only Judean, often felt estranged by language, custom, and tradition. It is common knowledge that the sense of separation is fertile soil for antisocial conduct. This explanation can be posited as one of the possible causes of the disaffection of Judas.

Also, Judas was a double-minded man. He is an illustration of the words of James, "What causes wars, and what causes fightings among you? Is it not your passions that are at war in your members?" By this analysis Judas was a man torn between love of the Master and love of money; desire to see the Kingdom of God come and ambition for his part in the Kingdom; love of the Lord and fear of what the pure eyes of the Lord saw in his wicked heart. This interpretation makes contact with modern psychological insights. Psychologists today emphasize the opposing forces that operate in man's personality. They tell us that much of our action results from inner conflicts that never rise to the level of conscious thought. All of this fits into the idea of Judas as a double-minded man and helps to make him a human being, understandable and possible.

Boyd Scott makes Judas a big man, a man of heroic temper, who chose deliberately the service of Satan. He compares Judas with the hero of John Davidson's *Triumph of Mammon*, who drew himself up and said:

> "Unarmed, condemned,
> The enemy of Christendom, I dare
> Your worst: I in the swept and garnished house
> Of that old faith the mouthing world is sick of,
> The proudest, rashest, sinfulest of men! . . .
> Who as he drave the dagger into the breast of his
> Father, King Christian, cried:
> 'Go up to Heaven! (stabs)
> Glare at me! Heart of Hell, what awful eyes!
> (stabs again)
> I would you were the soul of Christendom!
> (stabs a third time)
> I would you had been God!' "

"There is dreadful heroism here!" says Scott. "It blazes in the soul of Nietzsche, who called Christianity 'the foulest blot in the history of humanity.' Brave words! and these are great figures who are prepared to say, 'Evil, be thou my good!' It is in this gallery that Judas stands."

Boyd Scott's theory that Judas was a man of "mighty courage" who arrayed "himself openly and irrevocably with Satan" makes the struggle on Golgotha a conflict between God and Satan with Jesus and Judas the earthly representatives. It is great drama, but it overlooks the fact that Judas made no open attack on his Lord and was not known as a traitor until he kissed the

Master in the Garden of Gethsemane. In Scripture Judas is not the embodiment of evil doing battle with Jesus, the embodiment of good; he is simply an ordinary man who by ordinary processes of wrongdoing and false choices betrayed the Master.

Creators of fiction and folklore do not have to be limited to scriptural records. They are free to let their imaginations create as they wish. A first-century Coptic apocryphal gospel says that the wife of Judas, frantic with greed, egged him on to the betrayal of Christ for money to pay a gambling debt. A thirteenth-century English ballad has the same theme with the sister of Judas in the villain's role. A twelfth-century *Legenda Aurea* has Judas cast away in a chest at sea by his parents; years later, while in the service of Pontius Pilate, he marries a beautiful woman only to discover that she is his mother. So this ancient legend makes the Oedipus complex the basis of Judas' trouble. John Hayden in *The Faithless* gives Judas an unfaithful wife who goes off with another man.

Judas has been made guilty of almost every crime and wickedness known to man. Every new theory of evil is sooner or later used to explain his betrayal. This is quite natural, for the mystery of the man invites explanation. Some imagination or some extension of facts is necessary to make Judas real.

One of the popular theories to explain Judas was advanced by De Quincey in his *Studies on Sacred Records* published in 1857. De Quincey says that Judas believed that "Christ contemplated the establishment of a temporal kingdom—the restoration, in fact of David's throne; believing also that all the conditions toward the realization of such a scheme met and centered in the person of Christ." Judas came to believe that Christ was

> Sublimely over-gifted for purposes of speculation, but, like Shakespeare's great creation of Prince Hamlet, not correspondingly endowed for the business of action. . . . It became important, therefore, according to the view adopted by Judas, that his Master should be precipitated into action by a force from without, and thrown into the center of some popular movement, such as, once beginning to resolve, could not afterwards be suspended or checked. . . .

He fancied that by his vigor of action were fulfilled those great political changes which Christ approved, but wanted audacity to realize. His hope was, that, when at length actually arrested by the Jewish authorities, Christ would no longer vacillate: he would be forced into giving the signal to the populace of Jerusalem, who would then rise unanimously, for the double purpose of placing Christ at the head of an insurrectionary movement, and of throwing off the Roman yoke. . . .

The miscalculation, in fact, of Judas Iscariot . . . did not hinge at all upon political oversight, but upon a total spiritual blindness, however, he went no farther than at that time did probably most of his brethren . . . all alike imputing to their Master views utterly irreconcilable with the grandeur of his new and heavenly religion. . . . But whilst the other apostles had simply failed to comprehend their Master, Judas had presumptuously assumed that he did comprehend him; and understood his purposes better than Christ himself. His object was audacious in a high degree, but . . . for that very reason not treacherous at all.

According to De Quincey, Judas delivered Jesus up to the rulers not for money but to force him to take control of a revolution that would usher in the Kingdom of God. When events showed Judas his tragic error, in remorse he took his own life.

There are many variations of this central theme. Some suggest that the idea for forcing Jesus to begin a revolution by betraying him to the rulers was given to Judas by his Judean friends. Others suggest that Judas, looking for an earthly Kingdom that did not materialize, was moved by disillusionment to betray the Lord. The Jewish Scripture said, "When a prophet speaks in the name of the Lord, if the word does not come to pass or come true, that is a word which the Lord has not spoken; the prophet has spoken it presumptuously, you need not be afraid of him." Following this Scripture, Judas turned state's witness and got for himself what he could for his years of chasing shadows.

The emphasis in modern Bible study upon the expectation of a messianic earthly kingdom lends weight to these theories, which also commend themselves because they make of Judas an understandable, if tragic, character. Practically all modern fiction and drama rely on some variation of the theme that Judas was a mistaken patriot and that his betrayal was not traitorous but well intentioned.

There are certain weaknesses in De Quincey's portrait of Judas. How could anyone with Judas' high opinion of Jesus' power have such a low opinion of Jesus' wisdom and ability to act? How could Judas believe that the crisis he precipitated would change the character of Jesus? If before the betrayal Jesus was irresolute, indecisive, unable to act, how would his arrest suddenly transform him into the decisive positive character needed to lead a revolutionary movement?

The most serious weakness of De Quincey's portrait of Judas is that it has no support in Scripture. The Scripture pictures Judas as a traitor, a devil, a thief, a wicked man whose "office let another take," an enemy whose "habitation" shall "become desolate." The scriptural portrait of Judas needs some light to balance the darkness, some goodness to make believable his evil, but to change the scriptural villain into a mistaken patriot whose fault is "spiritual blindness" and "presumption" involves a reversal of character that does violence to the evidence of our only source of firsthand information. The mistaken-patriot view of Judas will continue to be popular, but it will never satisfy those who look to the Scripture for the key to the character of this apostle.

Judas remains a man of mystery. It is doubtful that a satisfactory understanding of him can be attained. No person is understandable unless the forces and motives at work in him are similar to those that operate in normal human beings. The ability to identify oneself with another is the basis of all understanding.

Edward G. Robinson acted the part of Rubashov in the prize-winning play *Darkness at Noon*. Rubashov was an ex-Communist who became disillusioned and changed sides. He was executed by the people that he tried to join.

This Rubashov [said Edward G. Robinson] is no villain. He is no worse than the rest of us. We are any and all characters. We are all people and all people are us. When an actor plays a role it is his commentary upon humanity. I am interested in the Rubashov that is in every man, just as I am interested in the little Julius Caesar that is in every man. We all tend to become these characters at times. What I like about this man is his great human side. The same vision that led him to become a Communist in the first place is also responsible for his ultimate disillusionment and defeat. I am a great believer in humanity.

John Bradford, the English divine, saw a man being led to the gallows and exclaimed, "There but for the grace of God, goes John Bradford." The spiritual imagination that gave birth to these often-quoted words enabled Bradford to understand and to help people.

The weakness of Judas did not set him apart from the Twelve. When our Lord said, "One of you will betray me," the disciples pointed each to himself and said, "Is it I?" Judas, perhaps to a greater degree than the other apostles, was activated by conflicting motives and forces that operate in all people. A recent magazine article tells of the self-sacrifice of inmates in American prisons who volunteer to be guinea pigs for medical experiments. For example, during World War II many combat areas were malaria-infested and our main supply of quinine was cut off. A Public Health Service team headed by Dr. G. Robert Coatney went to Atlanta Penitentiary and asked for volunteers to help find a new cure for malaria. The first day three hundred prisoners volunteered. Each man was infected by ten malaria-bearing mosquitoes. As the disease progressed the men were given no drugs until the fever was fully developed. More than thirty of them were hospitalized at one time with fevers running as high as 106 degrees. From these tests was developed chloroquinine (S.N. 7618), which proved to be more effective than quinine. Rushed to the battlefield, it saved many lives. Each volunteer received an emblem "Malaria Project" to wear on his sleeve. One volunteer refused his emblem, saying, "I don't want to touch it—this was the only decent thing I ever did."

Prisoners have volunteered to be guinea pigs in tests of syphilis, hepatitis, pellagra, common colds, skin disorders, and amoebic dysentery. In twelve state prisons and nine Federal prisons hundreds have volunteered for these hazardous experiments. Many inmates become so intersted that they volunteer for laboratory work or become nurses' aides, prison nurses, or prison technicians.

Dr. Austin McCormick, a leading prison authority, accounts for these volunteers by saying, "Prisoners volunteer chiefly because of a social conscience which many of them do not realize they have. Selfish motives play a secondary role. They welcome a chance to do some good to balance part of the harm they have done. Such projects boost the individual's morale enormously, and give the entire institution a lift."

Possibilities of evil go hand in hand with possibilities for good. The disciples had self-knowledge enough to admit that any of their number might have acted Judas' part. Their fingers did not point accusingly at him, saying, "Thou art a traitor." Each of them pointed to himself and asked, "Is it I?" The man who sees within himself the possibility of evil is the better protected from wrongdoing. The man who sees in himself the possibility of the sin of another is the man who can become the channel of grace to help others. If a man can see in the darkness of Judas one glimmer of the candle of goodness or in the bright goodness of his own soul can recognize some shadow of evil, then to him Judas can become a living, understandable human being.

Dante, the medieval genius, found no redeeming feature in Judas. A cold-blooded traitor, he did not deserve the mercy of Purgatory. Dante put him in the lowest hell, with his head in the very mouth of the Devil.

> "The soul up there which has the deepest pain,"
> The Master said, "is Judas Iscariot.
> With head inside, he plies his feet without."

By this judgment Dante made Judas the chief of sinners and his eternal torment the greatest in hell itself.

Robert Buchanan, who shares the modern distaste for placing

anyone in hell, has a ballad about Judas Iscariot which pictures Judas coming to the door of the Bridegroom in eternity:

> 'Twas the soul of Judas Iscariot stood black,
> and sad, and bare:
> "I have wandered many nights and days: there
> is no light elsewhere!"
>
> 'Twas the wedding-guests cried out within, and
> their eyes were fierce and bright—
> "Scourge the soul of Judas Iscariot away into
> the night!"
>
> 'Twas the Bridegroom stood at the open door,
> and beckoned, smiling sweet:
> 'Twas the soul of Judas Iscariot stole in, and
> fell at His feet.
>
> "The Holy Supper is spread within, and many
> candles shine;
> And I have waited long for thee before I poured
> the wine!"
>
> The Supper Wine is poured at last, the lights
> burn bright and fair;
> Iscariot washes the Bridegroom's feet, and dries
> them with his hair.

The Bible does not discuss the eternal fate of Judas. With characteristic reserve it says he went "to his own place." Following the example of Scripture, let us leave him to his own place and may God have mercy on his soul!

14

The Glorious Company

His gifts were that some should be
apostles,
some prophets,
some evangelists,
some pastors
and teachers.—EPHESIANS 4:11

THE TE DEUM PROCLAIMS THAT "THE GLORIOUS COMPANY of the apostles praise Thee." By their unique relationship with the Master, these men have exercised an influence on the Christian Church far beyond the sum total of their individual lives.

A primary contribution of the apostles to the Christian cause was the information about the life of Jesus they were able to supply to the Gospel writers. In the early Christian community no group lived so close to the Master over such a long period of time as did the apostles. It was to be expected that stories and teachings repeated by them should find their way into the Gospel record. As has been pointed out, Mark, the first Gospel writer, supposedly relied upon Peter as a source of information. Matthew and John no doubt had some part in recording the life of our Lord in the books that bear their names. Luke used many sources, both written and oral, and drew upon more than one of the apostles for his life of Jesus. A tendency developed in the early Christian Church so to spiritualize the Christ that the earthly life of Jesus was considered of small significance. Fortunately, the apostles did not share this view. Thanks to the help they gave the Gospel writers, the priceless record of the words and deeds of our Lord has been preserved.

But the apostles chosen by Jesus not only contributed information; they also set an example of true discipleship. The call given to Peter, Andrew, and the other disciples sounds across the ages as a call to modern disciples. The fears, failures, doubts, and vacillations of the apostles provide guidance for present-day Christians in their conflicts with like problems. The ideal fellowship described in John 14 is the goal for which true Christians still strive. The response of the apostles to the divine commission, "Go ye into all the world and preach the gospel to all creation," is the inspiration for all missionary endeavor. This ability of the apostles to leap from the pages of history and to walk the paths of contemporary life has never been better expressed than in the often-quoted words with which Dr. Albert Schweitzer closed his scholarly study *The Quest of the Historical Jesus:*

He comes to us as One unknown, without a name, as of old, by the lake side, he came to those men who knew him not. He speaks to us the same word: "Follow thou me," and sets us to the tasks which he has to fulfil for our time. He commands. And to those who obey him, whether they be wise or simple, he will reveal himself in the toils, the conflicts, the sufferings which they shall pass through in His fellowship, and, as an ineffable mystery, they shall learn in their own experience who he is.

A third power of these men who lived in the past to quicken life in the present is vividly captured by the artists who have painted the life of Jesus. Since the apostles played a part in practically every Gospel incident, the artists have of necessity placed them in their pictures of Jesus. The apostles represent in art the human response to the divine. The very humanity of the apostles makes the approach to the Master simple and effective; by imaginative identification with one of the Twelve, identification with the Master himself becomes easier. The apostolic symbols that adorn our churches in stained-glass windows, chancel carvings, and other sanctuary adornments also increase the impact of the apostles. Symbols speak to the deeper levels of life, directly touching the emotions. Recognizing this fact, previous generations at the time of baptism or confirmation of their children gave them apostolic spoons with the likeness of one of the apostles impressed on the handle, probably in the hope that the child would identify himself in a measure with that one apostle's life and teaching.

In the expression of faith as well as in the inspiration of art the apostles have an honored position. The most universal creed of the Church, the Apostles' Creed, gets its name from the tradition that it was composed phrase by phrase by the apostles. In many missals, as late as the fifteenth and sixteenth centuries, the Apostles' Creed was printed with the name of the apostle following the phrase for which he was thought to be responsible. This oft-repeated creed, which has entered so deeply into the mind of the Christian world, is assigned to the apostles as follows:

I believe in God, the Father Almighty,	Peter
Maker of heaven and earth;	John
and in Jesus Christ, his only Son our Lord;	James
who was conceived by the Holy Ghost, born of the Virgin Mary,	Andrew
suffered under Pontius Pilate, was crucified, dead, and buried;	Philip
He descended into hell; the third day He rose again from the dead;	Thomas
He ascended into heaven, and sitteth at the right hand of God the Father Almighty;	Bartholomew
from thence He shall come to judge the quick and the dead.	Matthew

I believe in the Holy Ghost, the Holy Catholic Church,	James, son of Alphaeus
the communion of saints; the forgiveness of sins;	Simon Zealot
the resurrection of the body;	Jude, son of James
and the life everlasting.	Matthias

By the middle of the second century the books which make up our New Testament were widely circulated and became the source of a common Christian tradition. No sooner were these books accepted by general usage than there began to appear apocryphal writing in the names of the apostles, pleading some point of view that was considered important or supplying by imagination unknown details of the life and action of the apostles. Following the literary divisions of the New Testament, these writings consisted of gospels assigned to Peter, Thomas, James, Philip, Bartholomew, and even Judas; acts designated Acts of John, Acts of Peter, Acts of Thomas, Acts of Andrew, Acts of Philip, and Acts of Thaddaeus; epistles of the apostles credited to the entire group of Christ's chosen; apocalypses entitled Revelation of Peter and Revelation of Thomas. These writings failed to win the approval of responsible church leaders but were exceedingly popular with the people. While some of them contain passages of value for their beauty of expression and moral teaching, for the most part the modern reader can be glad that time has removed them from general circulation. However, this vast literature is of interest because it shows the influence of the apostles in the life of the Christian Church during these early centuries. And the passage of time has in no way lessened their influence.

Since the beginning of the second century there have also appeared books which in the name of the apostles gave directions to the Church in matters relating to ritual and forms of worship. The authority of the apostles has, during the centuries, extended beyond these matters to include statements of binding faith and ecclesiastical structure that are believed to be the very foundation of the Church. This impact of the apostles is felt in our day by a significant group in the Christian fellowship. For instance, Dr. George Florovsky, the Greek Orthodox scholar, expresses this conviction thus:

> The Church exists by divine authority, and authority in the Church was committed to the Apostles who were divinely designated as its organs to exercise in it a permanent stewardship of grace and truth. Thus, not only was a Society established but it received the beginnings of a structure. The Church grew up round its Apostolic Ministry. There is a "given-ness" both in its faith and in its form. . . . The Church was no self-appointed or self-governing democracy. It acknowledged an abiding and directing constraint upon its freedom exercised by the Apostolic stewards whom Christ in the beginning set over His earthly household. This authoritative constraint manifests itself down the ages most noticeably in two connections, viz., in the Faith delivered through the Apostles, and in the historic ministry set within it from Apostolic days.

In language less theological Lesslie Newbigin, Bishop of the Church of South India, expresses doubt about the given-ness of a fixed faith but does firmly endorse a given-ness of spirit that forms the basis of apostolic authority for the Church.

> At the heart and center of the earthly ministry of the incarnate Christ was the choosing, training, and sending forth of a band of apostles. . . . He chose twelve men that they might be with Him and that He might send them forth. Being with Him they received, not so much a formal course of instruction in divine truth as an introduction into the intimacy of His Spirit. . . . And in sending them forth to teach and to have authority over the powers of evil, He gave them His own commission to represent His Person in the fullest sense. As He represents the Father, they are to represent Him in the world. . . . And because they are His apostles, they have His authority in the spiritual world. . . . This sense of unity, one may almost say of identity, of Jesus and His apostles, and indeed all who believe on Him through this word . . . indicates that there can be no question . . . that Jesus intended to be represented in all the plenitude of His power, by His own chosen and commissioned people.

This apostolic authority is accepted in varying degrees by the liturgical groups in the Protestant tradition, such as the Protestant Episcopal, the Greek Orthodox, and the Lutheran churches. Nonliturgical Protestant groups, such as the Presbyterian, Baptist, Methodist, and others, do not look to the apostles for such authority over the present-day church, but hold that a rigid given form and faith was the very thing against which Jesus protested in the religious life of his day. They stress direct communication of the individual spirit with God, looking upon the apostles as examples and guides rather than as a source of authority in ecclesiastical organization or dogma.

In the past, differences in interpretation of apostolic authority have been divisive factors; but today the issue is being reopened in the hope that apostolic authority can be restated in a form that will make it a basis of unity rather than division. In the United States the co-operative Christian movement has largely contented itself with action programs, giving little attention to theological issues. However, in the mission field, where major denominations have gone beyond co-operative action to organic union, discussion of apostolic authority has of necessity received serious attention. As a result the World Council of Churches, in contrast to the national and state councils in the United States, is actively discussing the meaning of apostolic authority in the hope of finding a common ground for deeper Christian fellowship.

All movements seek inspiration and guidance from their founding fathers, for, generally speaking, the central emphasis can be most clearly seen in the genesis of a movement. To return to the first Christian fellowship and to attempt to find the distinctive marks of apostleship should result in a quickening of spirit that will help fulfill our Lord's prayer that "they may be one."

Even a cursory reading of the New Testament reveals that there were leaders in the early Church who served with greater distinction than did some of the original Twelve. Paul was outstanding in intellectual ability; Apollos in oratorical skill; James, the brother of our Lord, in organizational leadership. The prominence of these later leaders does not invalidate the time-honored position of the apostles, who stand apart by the closeness of their fellowship with Jesus during his earthly life—a fellowship denied most of the other leaders, whose names do not appear in Scripture until after Pentecost. The apostles were Christ-chosen, Christ-ordained, and Christ-sent-forth. "You did not choose me," Jesus said to them, "but I chose you and appointed you that you should go and bear fruit."

It is almost as if our Lord reached his hand into the mass of God-loving men of Israel and came up with Twelve who were notable not so much for their difference from others as for their likeness to them. When the idea is pondered for a moment, the choice of common men, rather than men of genius, is seen as the highest wisdom. Paul said that God was always choosing "what is foolish in the world to shame the wise—what is weak to shame the strong—what is low and despised in the world, even things which are not, to bring to nothing things that are." The reason, he declared, is "that no human being might boast in the presence of God."

How indispensable is the common man! He runs the railroads, sails the seven seas, flies the airplanes, mans the factories, operates radio and television, cares for the sick, tills the soil, and performs the other ten thousand daily tasks that make up the workaday world. The president of a railroad may be sick and travel be unaffected, but no one moves if the engineers, switchmen, signalmen, or other key workers stay at home. Everyone is conscious of the importance of the scientist and research director in the modern world. Our prized gadgets and remarkable factories are products of their inventive genius. But equally remarkable are the skills in the hands of ordinary workmen on whom depend the ongoing work of the world. The skill of the common man separates civilization from savagery quite as much as does the knowledge of the scientist.

Our times have been called the steel age, the electric age, the air age, the atomic age. But a more discerning description of our age utilizes human instead of mechanical terms. This is the age of the common man. This age differs from the past in the importance it places on widespread education and specialized skills. Our age recognizes, as never before in history, the right of the common man to decide his own destiny. His opinion is more carefully sought and more closely followed today than in any previous era. No government, nor any policy of government, can long survive a hostile public opinion. Jesus recognized this importance of the common man when he called the Twelve to follow him.

It is characteristic of the common man to have an open heart and an open hand. Jesus called attention to the fact that when Elijah needed food he went to a widow who had only enough meal and oil for one scant dinner for herself and her son. The food shared in her extreme poverty sustained the prophet and her family during the famine. Again Jesus pointed out the widow who came timidly to the Temple treasury and cast in the only penny she possessed. He proclaimed her gift the greatest of all because others had cast in out of their abundance but she out of her poverty had cast in all that she had. How often the most needy are the most generous. The Church of Jesus Christ goes forward on sacrificial gifts of millions of people rather than on the generosity of the few who give millions of dollars. The forlorn child who needs a home is less apt to find an open door in a country estate than in a run-down cottage with a broken gate, dogs in the yard, cats on the ridgepole, and children all over the place. An injured man involved in an accident and left alone by the highway could ask no better fortune than to have a man with work-stained hands come his way. No hearts are more generous or hands more tender than the hearts and hands of those who, like the apostles, come from the common people.

To generosity must be added faithfulness. When the Cross threw its gaunt shadow the apostles were momentarily scattered, but soon they came together again never to part. Prison, fire, sword, persecution, peril—they endured all for His sake. In spite of all adversity and suffering those chosen by our Lord remained faithful. The faithfulness of common men to their daily work, their homes, their families, their church, and the other manifold obligations of life forms the solid foundation of social living. Men who do not go to sleep in the signal tower make it possible for trains to arrive safely at their destination. Women who care for home and children make it possible to have satisfying home life. Workers who faithfully perform monotonous, dangerous, or disagreeable tasks create great nations. Faithfulness is a workaday, drab virtue; but its value cannot be exaggerated.

There is an element of the heroic in the apostles. Their martyrdom is in most cases founded upon tradition, but the heroism of their daily lives is revealed in the Gospel stories. Courage is more often a potential than a spectacle. The average man who walks on the streets of any town, and who sits at the tables of millions of homes, has within him the possibilities of becoming a hero when occasion demands.

In the village of Hebron, Maryland, a mother left her four-year-old son in the automobile while she went into the post office. Somehow the child got the car started and it began to go around and around in a big circle, gathering speed until it crashed into another automobile and smashed a small pole supporting a porch. All who saw what was happening were frantic with fear. Someone sounded the fire alarm, adding to the confusion and danger. Finally, Carl Pollitt, Jr., a worker for the Wayne Pump Company, rushed to the car, held onto the handle of the door, broke the window with his fist, and reached in and turned off the switch. The child and the young man were unhurt. For a day the rescuer was a hero; the Lions Club presented him with a high-powered rifle at a banquet in his honor; but soon he was just Carl Pollitt, Jr., a worker for the Wayne Pump Company.

Identifying the apostles with common humanity enhances the true greatness of that "glorious company." It places the Gospel in proper perspective as a message for the many rather than the few. What God was able to accomplish with fishermen and tax collectors yesterday he can do with men in mills and markets today. If the Gospel changes men, it changes the world. This is the note of encouragement that comes from the select group who kept company with our Lord.

The last two chapters of the Bible describe the glory of the New Jerusalem that shall come from God to replace the strife, confusion, and suffering of the present world order. It is a glorious city which has no need of the sun or moon to shine upon it, for the glory of God is its light and the lamp thereof is the Lamb. Its gates are not shut by day and there is no night there. In this city there are no tears, no death, no mourning, nor crying, nor pain. The river of the water of life flows through the city. On each side of the river grows the tree of life, yielding its fruit each month, and the leaves of the tree are for the healing of the nations.

The walls of the city of God, the New Jerusalem, have Twelve foundations. On the foundation stones are graven the names of the Twelve apostles of the Lamb. Peter, Andrew, James, and John are there in company with Philip, Thomas, Matthew, and the others. The stones are living stones, human stones, and as such they share the inadequacies and limitations of all flesh. Each stone differs from the others, yet each has its important place in the Holy City of God.

Other foundation can no man lay than that which is laid. The Twelve apostles are a supreme example of what God can do with very human material that is yielded to his use. Their lives are an eternal inspiration and an ever-present example to all who love the Lord and seek to follow him.

"The glorious company of the apostles praise Thee." To their praise each Christian joins with glad and joyful hallelujahs, praying for the time when all mankind shall acknowledge Christ as King of kings and Lord of lords.

Sources

The Scripture references are to the Revised Standard Version of the Bible except when otherwise stated.

Chapter 1. *These Twelve*

PAGE	LINE	
1	15	I Cor. 1:2.
2	2	Acts 14:15.
3	2	Matt. 21:42.
4	29	Luke 4:1–2.
	30	Luke 9:29–36.
	31	Luke 22:41.
4	32	Luke 6:12.
5	1	Mark 3:14.
6	2	John 6:67, 68.
	9	Matt. 26:40.
	11	Mark 3:14.
7	2	Luke 6:12, 13.

Chapter 2. *Simon Peter, World-wide Fisherman*

PAGE	LINE	
8	1	Luke 5:1–11.
9	3	Matt. 14:22–33.
	31	Matt. 16:13–20.
10	8	John 1:42.
	9	Mark 3:16.
	10	Matt. 16:18.
	19	Matt. 16:19.
	35	Matt. 18:21.
11	1	Luke 12:41.
	2	Mark 10:28.
	3	Matt. 15:15.
	4	Mark 11:21.
	9	Mark 9:5, 6.
11	20	Luke 5:8, Matt. 14:29.
	21	Luke 9:33.
	22	John 20:1–6.
	24	John 21:7, 8.
	33	Mark 14:37.
12	3	John 18:10.
	17	Matt. 16:11–23.
	33	Luke 22:24–27.
13	8	John 13:3–9.
	20	Matt. 26:30–35.
	29	Matt. 26:72; Luke 22:61, 62.

PAGE	LINE	
14	8	Mark 8:33; Luke 22:45.
	10	Matt. 16:23; Mark 14:37; Matt. 26:40.
	11	Luke 24:34; I Cor. 15:5.
	22	Mark 8:31–33.
	23	Luke 22:61.
	25	John 21:15–19.
15	9	Matt. 16:13.
	11	John 21:15–19.
	19	Acts 12:2–17.
	22	Acts 15:1–22.
	32	Gal. 2:9.
16	5	Acts 2:14–40.
	14	Acts 3:12–26.
	16	Acts 4:8–12; 10:34–43.
	17	Acts 11:5–17.
	18	Acts 15:7–11.
	26	Acts 3:1–6; 5:15.
	27	Acts 8:14; 9:32; 10:24, 25; 12:19; 4:3; 12:5.
	28	Acts 5:40; 8:14, 15.
	29	Acts 5:1–5.
17	3	Acts 1:15–26.
	14	Gal. 2:12.
	26	Acts 15.
	32	Acts 2:7.
18	1	Acts 8:4–8.
	14	Acts 8:14–16.
	19	Acts 10.
19	12	Acts 11:1–18.
	21	Acts 10:34.
	29	Acts 13:1–4.
19	35	Acts 14:27.
20	1	Acts 15:1, 2.
	18	Acts 15:8–11.
	24	Acts 15:23–30.
	33	Gal. 2:11, 12.
21	3	Acts 15.
	6	Acts 10:34.
	14	I Pet. 3:10.
	15	I Pet. 4:2.
	16	I Pet. 5:8.
	17	I Pet. 2:4–10.
	27	Fragments of Papias III, 15, in *The Apostolic Fathers* (Fathers of the Church Series, Vol. IV), trans. Francis X. Glimm, Joseph M. F. Marique, S.J., and Gerald G. Walsh, S.J. (New York: Cima Publishing Co., 1947), p. 377.
22	18	I Clement, Chaps. 5 and 6, in *The Apostolic Fathers,* Vol. IV, pp. 13, 14.
	33	Acts of Peter XXXV, in M. R. James, *The Apocryphal New Testament* (London: Oxford University Press, 1953), p. 333.

PAGE	LINE	
23	15	F. J. Foakes-Jackson, *Peter: Prince of the Apostles* (New York: George H. Doran Co., 1927), p. 254.

Chapter 3. *Andrew, the Friend*

PAGE	LINE	
24	1	John 1:35–40.
25	7	Matt. 3:2, 3.
26	6	John 1:41, 42.
	22	John 6:4–11.
27	21	John 12:20–26.
28	16	Quoted in full in *New Schaff-Herzog Encyclopedia of Religious Knowledge* (New York and London: Funk & Wagnalls Co., 1910), Vol. 8, p. 56.
	33	Matt. 10:2.
29	11	Mark 5:37; Matt. 17:1; 26:37.

Chapter 4. *James, the First Apostolic Martyr*

PAGE	LINE	
35	15	John 1:35–42.
	23	Mark 1:16–20; Matt. 4:18–22; Luke 5:1–11.
36	5	Luke 5:1–11.
	23	Luke 5:27, 28; John 1:43–51.
	35	Matt. 4:23 to 10:1.
37	9	Luke 6:12, 13.
	17	Matt. 10:5–15.
	22	Matt. 10:16–23.
38	7	Mark 3:17.
	14	Mark 15:40.
	17	Matt. 27:56.
	20	John 19:25.
39	1	Mark 5:22; 9:2; 14:33.
39	7	Mark 3:17.
	10	Luke 9:54.
	19	Mark 10:35–45.
	28	Charles R. Brown, *These Twelve* (New York: Harper & Brothers, 1926), p. 25.
	34	A. Boyd Scott, *The Twelve Take Stock of Us* (New York: George H. Doran Co., 1925), p. 19.
40	16	Acts 1:13.
	27	Acts 12:1–2.

PAGE	LINE	
41	14	Rom. 15:28.
41 ff.		For traditions about James, see S. J. Stone, *The Cult of Santiago* (London: Longmans Green & Co., 1927).
47	31	Eusebius Pamphili, *Ecclesiastical History,* Bks. I–V (Fathers of the Church Series, Vol. 19), trans. Roy J. Deferrari (New York: Fathers of the Church, Inc., 1953), Bk. II, Chap. 9, p. 99.

CHAPTER 5. *John, Beloved Son of Thunder*

PAGE	LINE	
49	5	Mark 9:38–40.
50	6	Luke 9:51–56.
	14	Mark 10:35–45, paraphrased.
51	19	Mark 5: 22–24; 5:35–43.
	21	Luke 9:28–36.
	26	Luke 22:8.
52	10	John 13:21–26.
	15	John 18:15.
	18	John 19:25–27.
	25	John 20:2–9.
	33	John 21:7.
53	3	John 21:15–23.
	31	Eusebius Pamphili, *Ecclesiastical History,* Vol. 2, Bks. VI ff., trans. Kirsopp Lake (London: William Heinemann; New York: G. P. Putnam's Sons, 1926), Bk. VI, Chap. 14, v. 7, p. 49.
54	22	John 4:24.
	24	John 6:63.
	26	John 11:25, 26.
	29	John 14:1–3.
	34	John 6:35.
55	1	John 3:16.
	7	I John 3:18.
	9	I John 3:14.
	13	I John 4:7.
	16	I John 4:21.
	17	I Cor. 13.
	33	Archibald M. Hunter, *Interpreting the New Testament 1900–1950* (Philadelphia: Westminster Press, 1951). Consult for a good brief summary of this problem and

PAGE	LINE	
55		reasons for accepting the intermediate position.
56	15	John 1:2, 3.
	28	Acts 1:13.
	29	Acts 2.
	35	Acts 3:4–19.
57	1	Acts 4:3–22.
	8	Acts 4:19.
	11	Acts 5:18–21.
	16	Acts 6:9–7:58.
	23	Acts 8:14–18.
58	4	Acts 15:1–21.
	13	D. A. Hayes, *John and His Writing* (New York: Methodist Book Concern, 1917), pp. 35, 41.
58	18	Eusebius, *op. cit.*, Bk. V, Chap. 24, v. 3, p. 335.
	22	Fragments of Papias V, in *The Apostolic Fathers*, p. 376.
59	27	Eusebius, *op. cit.*, Bk. III, Chap. 23, p. 170.
60	16	Jerome, Commentary on Galatians VI:10, *Catholic Encyclopedia* (New York: Robt. Appleton Co., 1910), Vol. 8, p. 493.

CHAPTER 6. *Philip of Bethsaida*

61	19	John 1:44.
63	1	John 1:43.
	13	John 1:45.
	28	John 6:1–14.
	34	John 6:7, paraphrased.
64	15	John 14:1–11, paraphrased.
65	18	John 1:43–46.
66	24	John 12:20–36.
67	1	Luke 22:42.
	14	John 14:8.
68	8	Eusebius, Vol. I, trans. Kirsopp Lake, *op. cit.*, Bk. V, Chap. 24. v. 3, p. 505.
	15	Acts of Philip, in James, *op. cit.*, pp. 439–49.
	32	John 1:44.
	33	Mark 1:21, 29.
	34	Luke 9:10.
	35	Matt. 14:13; John 6:1; Mark 6:45.
	37	Alfred Edersheim, *The Life and Times of Jesus the Messiah* (New York: E.

PAGE	LINE	
68		R. Herrick Co., 1886), Vol. I, pp. 88, 677; Vol. II, pp. 3 ff.
69	3	B. Harvie Branscomb, "The Gospel of Mark," in *The Moffatt New Testament Commentary* (New York: Harper & Brothers, 1913), p. 117.

CHAPTER 7. *Nathanael Bartholomew*

PAGE	LINE	
70	9	Matt. 10:2–4; Mark 3:16–19; Luke 6:14–16; Acts 1:13.
	12	John 1:43–51.
71	30	Arnold J. Toynbee, *A Study of History,* abr. D. C. Somervell (New York: Oxford University Press, 1947), p. 217.
72	10	*The Confessions of St. Augustine,* trans. Edward B. Pusey (New York: Pocket Books, Inc.), p. 147.
76	11	Acts of Philip, in James, *op. cit.,* pp. 439–49.
	22	Eusebius, trans. Roy J. Deferrari, *op. cit.,* Bk. V, Chap. 10, v. 4, p. 303.

CHAPTER 8. *Matthew, the Tax Collector*

PAGE	LINE	
83	3	Matt. 3:2, 3.
	9	Luke 3:12, 13; Matt. 3:7.
	12	Mark 1:21–2:12.
84	22	Matt. 9:9.
	29	Matt. 9:10–13.
86	16	Matt. 9:9; Mark 2:14.
87	5	Luke 5:31.
87	10	John 8:11; Matt. 9:13; Hos. 6:6.
	31	Luke 15:11–32.
89	32	Luke 7:36–50.
90	20	Francis Thompson, "The Hound of Heaven," as quoted in *The*

PAGE	LINE	
90	20	*World's Great Religious Poetry,* ed. Caroline Miles Hill (New York: The Macmillan Co., 1923), p. 45. Used by permission of the Lane Publishing Co., Menlo Park, Calif.
91	26	Acts 1:13.
92	13	Carl A. Glover, *With the Twelve* (Nashville: Abingdon-Cokesbury Press, 1939), p. 224.
	19	Matt. 2:6; 2:15; 2:17; 2:23; 3:3; 4:14, etc.
	26	Matt. 1:17.
	31	Matt. 13:44, 45.
	34	Matt. 6:25.
	36	Matt. 16:26.
93	2	Matt. 19:24.
	5	Matt. 2:1–12.
	12	Matt. 28:20.
	20	Eusebius, *op. cit.,* Bk. III, Chap. 39, v. 15, p. 206.
	34	Edgar J. Goodspeed, *The Twelve: The Story of Christ's Apostles* (Philadelphia; John C. Winston Co., 1957), p. 86.

CHAPTER 9. *Doubting Thomas*

PAGE	LINE	
94	15	John 20:25.
95	19	Thornton B. Penfield, Jr., *My Name Is Thomas* (Philadelphia: Magee Press, 1937), p. 7.
	31	John 11:16; 20:24.
96	6	John 11:1–16.
97	21	John 10:40.
	23	John 8:59.
	26	John 10:31.
98	3	John 11:54.
	19	Luke 9:51, K.J.
99	7	John 14:1–4.
	15	John 14:5.
	17	John 14:6.
100	19	Sir Oliver Lodge, quoted in Robert Freeman, *What of the Twelve?* (New York: Doubleday, Doran & Co., 1929), p. 130.
101	8	Penfield, *op. cit.,* p. 10. Used with permission.

PAGE	LINE	
101	23	John 20:14.
	25	John 20:19.
	26	John 20:24.
	28	John 20:25.
	31	John 20:26–29.
102	7	Mark 16:9–11.
	12	Mark 16:12, 13.
	16	Mark 16:14.
	22	Luke 24:11.
103	10	John 20:29.
	23	E. A. Wallis Budge, *Baralam and Yĕwâsĕf,* "The Acts of St. Thomas the Apostle to India" (London: Cambridge University Press, 1923), p. 298. Used with permission.
105	15	Hazel E. Foster in *The Christian Century* (Chicago), Nov. 5, 1952.
107	21	Budge, *op. cit.,* p. 314. Used with permission.

CHAPTER 10. *James, the Son of Alphaeus*

PAGE	LINE	
109	8	Matt. 10:2–4.
	15	Matt. 27:56.
	16	Luke 23:55–24:1.
110	13	Mark 15:40.
	14	John 19:25.
	28	Matt. 10:3.
	28	Mark 2:14.
111	1	Mark 15:40.
112	9	Rufus Jones, *Finding the Trail of Life* (New York: The Macmillan Company, 1926), pp, 21, 22.
	31	E. C. Urwin, *Can the Family Survive?* (London: Student Christian Movement Press, 1944), p. 122.
113	32	Theodore Roosevelt, *Theodore Roosevelt's Letters to His Children,* ed. Joseph B. Bishop (New York: Charles Scribner's Sons, 1919), pp. 75, 76
114	36	*The Prudential Family,* Feb., 1951, Vol. 2, No. 1 (Newark: Prudential Insurance Co.). Used with permission.

PAGE	LINE	
115	36	J. D. Jones, *The Glorious Company of the Apostles* (London: James Clarke & Co., 1904), p. 221.
116	1	Matt. 13:55.
	9	John 7:5.
	10	I Cor. 15:7.
	19	Eusebius, *op. cit.*, Bk. II, Chap. 23, v. 5, p. 125.
117	10	Gospel according to the Hebrews, in James, *op. cit.*, p. 3.
	24	Eusebius, *op. cit.*, Bk. II, Chap. 23, v. 13 ff., p. 126.
118	6	Eusebius, *op. cit.*, Bk. II, Chap. 23, v. 24, p. 128.

CHAPTER 11. *Simon, the Zealot*

PAGE	LINE	
119	2	Luke 6:15; Acts 1:13.
	3	Matt. 10:4; Mark 3:18.
121	3	Luke 23: 16, 20, 23.
	8	Acts 26:32.
	31	Luke 13:1.
	35	Acts 5:36, 37.
122	1	Luke 23:14–19.
123	5	Rom. 13:1, K.J.
	25	I Macc. 2:50, 51.
125	4	Josephus, *Wars of the Jews,* trans. William Whiston (London: W. Boyer, 1737; reprinted 1902), Vol. 4, Bk. 4, Chap. 6.
	21	Matt. 22:15 ff.
	26	Luke 13:34, 35.
	29	Luke 19:42–44.

CHAPTER 12. *Judas, Son of James*

PAGE	LINE	
128	8	Tracy D. Mygatt and Frances Witherspoon, *The Glorious Company* (New York: Harcourt, Brace & Co., 1928), p. 117.
129	10	Matt. 10:3, K.J.
	11	Mark 3:18; Luke 6:16.
	16	John 14:22.

PAGE	LINE	
129	34	John 13:3 ff.
130	15	I Cor. 11:23–26.
	28	John 15.
	29	John 16.
	30	John 17.
	34	John 14.
131	19	John 14:22.
132	8	James E. Cranshaw, *The Supreme Grace* (London: Charles H. Kelley, 1910), p. 110.
	34	Matt. 22:37–39.
133	4	I Cor. 1:12.
	8	I Cor. 5:1.
	10	I Cor. 6:1.
	12	I Cor. 11:20, 21.
	17	I Cor. 13:1–14:1.
	23	John 14:23.
	34	Matt. 28:20.
134	2	John 14:27.
	7	John 16:33.
	20	John 14:28.
	29	John 11:36.
135	4	John 20:16.
	10	John 14:30.
	23	Matt. 26:39.
	25	Matt. 27:46.
135	28	John 19:11.
	31	Luke 23:46.
136	6	Paul Geren, *The Pilgrimage of Peter Strong* (New York: Harper & Brothers, 1948), pp. 112, 113. Used with permission.
137	31	Jude 1:1.
	34	Jude 1:17, 18
138	8	Eusebius, *op. cit.*, Bk. I, Chap. 13, p. 78. Quoted as recorded in Myrtle Strode Jackson, *Lives and Legends of the Apostles and Evangelists* (London: Lutterworth Press, 1928), p. 120. Used with permission.
139	30	Goodspeed, *op. cit.*, pp. 21, 41.

Chapter 13. *Judas Iscariot*

PAGE	LINE	
141	7	Matt. 26:49.
	8	Luke 22:48.
	17	John 6:70.
142	27	John 13:30.
143	12	Luke 3:30.
	13	Matt. 13:55; Acts 1:13.
	14	Acts 5:37.

PAGE	LINE	
143	16	Acts 9:11.
	17	Acts 15:22.
	22	Luke 6:13.
144	6	John 6:64.
	9	Alexander Balmain Bruce, *The Training of the Twelve* (New York: Doubleday, Doran & Co., 1929), p. 369.
	31	John 12:6.
145	13	Matt. 26:14.
	14	I Tim. 6:10.
	24	Amos 2:6.
146	1	J. D. Jones, *op. cit.*, p. 252.
147	5	John 12:1–8.
	13	Matt. 26:6–13; Mark 14:3–9.
	18	Matt. 16:23.
	23	John 6:70.
	26	John 6:71.
148	3	John 13:26.
	4	Leslie Weatherhead, *His Life and Ours* (London: Hodder & Stoughton, Ltd., 1932), p. 236.
	9	John 13:27.
	32	Jas. 4:1.
149	9	John Davidson, *Triumph of Mammon*, quoted in Scott, *op. cit.*, p. 148. Used with permission.
150	16	John Hayden, *The Faithless* (New York: Samuel French, Inc., 1938).
	30	Thomas De Quincey, *Theological Essays* (Boston: Ticknor, Reed, and Fields, 1857), Vol. 1, Chap. "Judas Iscariot."
151	28	Deut. 18:22.
152	14	Luke 6:16; John 6:70; 12:6.
	15	Acts 1:20.
	35	*Baltimore Sun*, Oct. 4, 1951.
153	15	Matt. 26:21, 22.
	19	"A Treasure in Every Heart," *Reader's Digest*, Dec., 1954.
154	30	Dante, *Inferno*, Canto XXXIV.
155	3	Robert Buchanan, ballad quoted by Scott, *op. cit.*, p. 143. Used with permission.
	24	Acts 1:25.

CHAPTER 14. *The Glorious Company*

PAGE	LINE	
157	26	Albert Schweitzer, *The Quest of the Historical Jesus. A Critical Study of Its Progress from Reimarus to Wrede,* trans. W. Montgomery (New York: The Macmillan Company, 1926), p. 401.
159	8	For a summary of these books see Goodspeed, *op. cit.,* p. 103 ff.; for full text of the same, see James, *op. cit.*
160	5	George Florovsky, *Man's Disorder and God's Design,* one-vol. ed. (New York: Harper & Brothers), p. 62.
	22	Lesslie Newbigin, *The Household of God* (New York: Friendship Press, 1954), p. 62.
	30	John 17:22.
162	6	John 15:16.
	15	I Cor. 1:27–29.
163	12	Luke 4:26.
	15	Luke 21:2.
165	15	Rev. 21:14.

Set in Intertype Baskerville
Format by Norma Stahl
Manufactured by The Haddon Craftsmen, Inc.
Published by HARPER & BROTHERS, *New York*